CONTEN

CW00760617

A Gnostic Biography of the Butthole Surfers

Ben Graham

Published by
Eleusinian Press Ltd
www.eleusinianpress.co.uk

Printed and bound in Great Britain by
Copytech (UK) Ltd

A catalogue record for this book
is available from The British Library

ISBN 978-1-909494-16-9

1
TOO MUCH ACID

The Butthole Surfers roared out of Texas like a tornado of brutal, ugly noise, surrealist free association, sick humour and rampant, anti-establishment chaos that had also swept up random ruined fragments of rock history, a whole bunch of wild props and costumes, the detritus of 20th century avant-garde art and, almost accidentally, moments of real human tenderness and significance that were all too easy to miss as they hurtled by. Though initially considered a punk band, they were in fact far more than just that; in many ways they were also a continuation of the acid-driven psychedelic movement that had peaked over a decade before they formed, and which by the late seventies was considered by most of the younger generation to be an anachronism and an embarrassment.

Certainly, the Butthole Surfers formed in the immediate aftermath of punk rock and – at least at first – identified largely as punks, as much out of self-deprecation and hatred of pretension as anything else. All of their initial shows and support were from within the punk scene, and when the Butthole Surfers have been written about, they've generally been judged against punk standards. As a result, whenever they've breached the unwritten punk code of conduct – which they did most spectacularly by taking legal action against the indie record label that put out their early albums – they've been condemned more harshly than any non-punk band might be for taking the same course of action.

Yet the Butthole Surfers were always an awkward fit within the punk scene. Yes, punk inspired them, and yes, punk bands gave them support gigs, and punk kids came to their shows when literally no-one else would have them. But what the Butthole Surfers were doing at those shows, from the beginning, was almost without precedent. One has to look a lot further back than Black Flag or the Dead Kennedys, the Sex Pistols or the Ramones, to find the roots of the Butthole Surfers.

Dada was an art movement that sprang up loosely in reaction to the First World War – or, more precisely, in reaction to the forces that were thought to have led to the First World War, in all its pointless horror and protracted agony. Those forces were identified as bourgeois conformism, mainstream culture, rational thinking, accepted wisdom, conventional morality and existing social, political and financial structures. Against these monoliths, Dada deployed irrational acts, deliberately shocking statements and behaviour, nonsense, clowning, provocation, satire, and magic. Many of their ideas were later formalised, and arguably commercialised, as surrealism. If Dada was punk, then surrealism was new wave, and punk itself could be seen as a reiteration of the original Dada spirit (as argued by critic Greil Marcus in his influential book, *Lipstick Traces*).

The Butthole Surfers brought the Dada elements of punk out into the open. They weren't just shocking and provocative because they couldn't play particularly well, and made a loud, uncompromising noise, and said rude and angry things in their lyrics; though this was as true of them as it was of a thousand other punk bands. The Butthole Surfers were also ridiculous – head-spinningly so. They were frequently naked, or on fire, or pinned up in dozens of clothes pegs, pissing and shitting on the stage. If there was a sensibility to be offended, they offended it, all the while crafting an increasingly disorienting environment around them onstage, to the extent that they didn't just rage against consensus reality, they appeared to come from (and drag their audiences into) another universe altogether, one where all of the old rules and assumptions just didn't apply.

This was absolute freedom, the American dream taken to its furthest frontier. But as Jack Nicholson said in *Easy Rider,* talking about freedom is one thing, but you show most people what true freedom really looks like and they get scared and dangerous. The Butthole Surfers' idea of freedom was frightening, and alienating to many. This was a world where anything could happen, and where all manner of influences and entities could potentially be channelled and come through.

The Butthole Surfers themselves would deny all of this, of course. They would say that the props, the light shows and the absurdist theatre were all just ways of distracting from the fact that they couldn't play and that their songs were bullshit. Leaving aside the fact that by the time they hit their prime all of the Butthole Surfers were competent, road-hardened musicians, and that Paul Leary in particular was one of the most innovative guitar players of his generation; the Buttholes' continued insistence that their band was always a scam and their songs meaningless pieces of crap – at best bad jokes at the expense of most rock fans' credulity and lack of taste – is a symptom of their understandable fear that a creative process whereby great works of art are generated almost randomly and without conscious effort, or even conscious understanding, from the subconscious psyche might be analysed too closely.

This is the point at which Dada meets magic, and where the Butthole Surfers most clearly depart from the punk template, which, for all its insistence on the value of chaos, generally favours disciplined songwriting, direct, unambiguous messages and a coherent unity of image and approach. The Butthole Surfers, by contrast, apparently don't know what they're doing – and, as a result, create great art that is truly transcendental, possessing a power they neither intended nor fully understand.

In this book I've written at length about the Butthole Surfers' albums, in most cases analysing them song by song. Some would say that this is the wrong approach – that the Butthole Surfers were all about the live experience, and that the records are just the ephemeral debris left in their wake. But the further we get from the Buttholes' actual lifespan as a working band, the more the records are really all we have left to tell their story, and the more they grow as works of art in their own right.

Many might say too that I've over-analysed the songs, reading things into them that were clearly never intended. I suggest that, to some extent, intention is beside the point. The point is that these things *can* be read into them; that the song, or more precisely the recording, is capable of supporting far more than its creators ever realised. On several occasions I've talked about the records in terms of alchemy and magic. I think that this is appropriate, because these are the tools with which mankind has traditionally voyaged into the collective unconsciousness, bringing back strange and unbelievable prizes. Operating through the medium of toilet jokes and gross sexual puns, the Butthole Surfers have inadvertently brought forth nuggets of great universal wisdom; they have performed scatological alchemy, and have turned shit into gold.

This gnostic interpretation of the band's work forms the heart of this book. Alongside a straightforward history drawn from existing sources, I've gone deep into the Butthole Surfers' body of work to bring back personal insights that will hopefully further illuminate their odyssey. Gibby Haynes and Paul Leary may not be 'great' songwriters in the accepted sense, although Gibby is capable of breathtaking lyrical streams of consciousness that yield many deathlessly memorable lines, and Paul, as noted, is a guitar player with an impressive technical and emotional range. But, together with their bandmates, they created recordings like black holes; mysterious gateways to other universes with their own strange gravity which, when closely approached, are truly mind-bending and psychedelic.

Contrary to popular clichés, psychedelia has never been just about love, peace and flowers, especially not in Texas. The psychedelic journey, with its moments of ego death and apocalyptic revelation, can be harsh and brutal, if also frequently hilarious. The ongoing moment of attempting to reintegrate your psychedelically enlightened self with the unyielding strictures of society can also present its fair share of difficulties. Every tripper can begin to feel like an unwitting Dadaist.

Texas has a special place in psychedelic history. The mythology of the place favours absolute independence by any means necessary, the romance of the outlaw, and a commitment to exploration and expansion towards the final frontier, whether that be the cowboy dream of pushing west or Houston's mission to the stars. The state's early pioneering psychedelic explorers were outlaws, pushing back the frontiers of consciousness even as they pushed at the limits of what the law would tolerate in terms of individual freedom. Even before the advent of LSD, Texas had supplied the powerful psychedelic peyote cactus for those brave enough to risk the nausea that accompanied its visions, and the vast desert landscape that was never far away was enough in itself to encourage cosmic epiphanies.

One of the most important (if perennially underrated) psychedelic bands of the 1960s was Austin's own 13th Floor Elevators. Formed in the mid-sixties by jug player, lyricist and acid evangelist/mastermind Tommy Hall, their not-so-secret weapon was the searing voice and presence of singer Roky Erickson, alongside doomed, understated guitar hero Stacy Sutherland. The Elevators were allegedly the first band to use the term 'psychedelic' to describe their music, dropped acid at every gig, and did their best to convey the full LSD experience through their songs and performances. While Hall attempted to compress the vivid rush of psychedelic illumination into the lyrics of songs like 'Slip Inside This House', Roky's howling banshee renditions and the raw garage attack of the band (especially with their original rhythm section) accurately conveyed the existential terror, panic and confusion that a heavy trip can also entail.

This confrontational aspect to the Elevators' shows, and their unwillingness to dress the psychedelic experience up in the chiffon and lace of pre-Raphaelite fashion, was the main reason they bombed when they played San Francisco's ballrooms before the self-styled 'beautiful people' of the west coast. Dressed in jeans, boots and plaid work shirts, the Elevators more resembled the grunge bands of two decades later than the hippy aristocracy of the late sixties. For one thing you just couldn't get away with that shit in 1960s Texas. Even as it was the Elevators – along with contemporaries such as the Golden Dawn, the Zakary Thaks, the Lost and Found and more – were constantly harassed by the authorities, the police and assorted rednecks. The positive effect of this, however, was that it toughened up the bands' sounds, so that Texan psychedelia became characterised by a snotty, kick-ass punk element, just as it delved deeper into the authentic acid experience than any of the more widely successful strains of the music.

The Elevators disintegrated at the end of their decade, screwed by their record company, ripped off by their admirers, and harassed into decades of mental illness, incarceration, drug addiction, poverty and – in the case of guitarist Stacy Sutherland – a stupid, tragic, violent early death. Their cult would grow in their absence, but if any band can be said to have carried the spirit of Texan psychedelia into the cold, dead-eyed decade of Ronald Reagan's 1980s, then it is surely the Butthole Surfers. Although they emerged from the hardcore punk scene and their act incorporated elements of industrial noise, performance art and, eventually, even hip-hop and electronica, the Buttholes' twisted, blackened heart always truly belonged to psychedelia – albeit of a distinctly nightmarish variety.

Consider the evidence. The Surfers' music – as often a mutant, unstable strain of haunting folk-rock as all-out noise assault – is disorienting, disturbing and sometimes even strangely beautiful. Frequently quoting late sixties/early seventies rock classics, the Buttholes consistently performed covers of older psych-related artists like Black Sabbath and Donovan, drawing out their full hallucinogenic horror. Their sick sense of humour is as surreal as it is scatological, the lyrical imagery enhanced by the trippy effects that layer the vocals of their singer, the wild-eyed, so-smart-he-has-to-be-crazy, feral maniac that is Gibby Haynes.

To the Buttholes and their audience, old-style hippy utopianism seemed hopelessly naïve and outdated. Reacting against the War on Drugs and the new Puritanism that characterised the latter days of the Cold War, in which the nuclear terror was dulled by escalating consumerism, trash culture and an ever-widening gap between rich and poor, all they could do was howl and rage in mockery and protest, at the same time as their Dadaist performances strove to break down the social conditioning that allowed the acceptance of those outrages in the first place.

Live, the band always aimed for a visual and sensory overload that recalled the lightshows of San Francisco bands like the Jefferson

Airplane and the Grateful Dead, but hyper-driven to blow the minds of the jaded, cynical post-punk generation. Utilising a formidable battery of strobe lights and smoke machines alongside multiple projections of medical operations and road accidents, spliced with old episodes of *Charlie's Angels* or nature footage, the band would set fire to the stage and tear stuffed animals to pieces as Gibby shook dozens of clothes pegs from his hair, firing them into the audience, or screamed through a bullhorn, or stripped off to simulate sex with naked dancer Kathleen, AKA Ta-dah the Shit Lady. And, of course, the Butthole Surfers were no strangers to drugs, both for inspiration and recreation, taking to the stage while on acid almost as often as the Elevators had.

As the band's notoriety spread, it became *de rigeur* for the audience to also drop acid at a Buttholes' show, in order to experience its full impact. Buttholes fans were not the booze and speed freaks of the hardcore scene, and certainly not the straight edgers who attended shows by bands like Minor Threat on nothing stronger than soda pop and candy bars. The Butthole Surfers engendered a whole new psychedelic subculture, at a time when LSD use had fallen markedly out of favour, thanks to its association with the failures and delusions of the by-then embarrassingly middle-aged, tie-dyed Woodstock generation.

"Finally the punk rockers are taking acid," someone once said of the Flaming Lips, who used the phrase as the title of a compilation of their early work. They were minor contemporaries of the Butthole Surfers, whose eventual rise to fame and fortune came about at roughly the same time as the Butthole's decline and disappearance from the scene. In their earliest incarnation the Flaming Lips owed much to the Buttholes' template: using a similar mix of noise, surrealism, acid rock, punk and the avant-garde, they carved out a formidable underground reputation before launching themselves at the mainstream. Like the Butthole Surfers, the Lips were known for their wild, immersive and senses-deranging live show; like Gibby, head Lip Wayne Coyne would holler through a bullhorn while explosions, props and costumed dancers bombarded the audience from all sides.

Ultimately, however, the Flaming Lips were a much more acceptable proposition to the music industry and to mainstream audiences than the Butthole Surfers. Their anatomical references were somewhat more restrained and their songwriting would become increasingly gentle and melodic, with nihilism and shock-Dada approaches gradually replaced by messages of love, peace and hope that bordered on the cloyingly sentimental. Coyne adopted a wide-eyed shaman-clown persona that mixed childlike innocence with old man wisdom, and was as safe and unthreatening as similar familiar archetypes long deployed in family-friendly Hollywood movies. Coyne would be allowed to go places where Gibby Haynes' acid-tripping transvestite serial killer would instantly find himself debarred.

By the mid-'00s, the Butthole Surfers had all but vanished into ignominy, and the Flaming Lips were standard-bearers for a new wave of psychedelic bands that produced some good music while still seeming toothless and nostalgic in comparison to their predecessors. Groups like the Black Angels and Thee Oh Sees slotted easily into an accepted alt-rock template, and conjured psychedelic sounds via the knowing deployment of ready-loaded imagery and an infinite selection of effects pedals. Further underground, the likes of Comets On Fire and Sunburned Hand Of The Man were more genuinely freaky, but none of these acts communicated the very real danger and shock of the unknown that the Butthole Surfers doled out in spades at their mid-eighties peak.

The Butthole Surfers threw themselves into the fire. In their music as in their lives, they went right to the edge, and then they went over it. They were America's last great psychedelic band. They went further than the Elevators, Hendrix, the Airplane, the Dead, the Velvets, or any great 'out-there' sixties group you care to name, and staked out a frontier that those that came after are still tentatively inching towards, or else nervously retreating from. There was never another band like them, and there never will be. They were punks, artists, explorers and magicians, anointing you with the piss wands of their incontinent genius. Ladies and gentlemen, I give you the Butthole Surfers. And may god have mercy upon your souls.

2
THE PEPPERMINT PUNK

Our story begins not in the heart of Texas, but its damp and humid crotch. San Benito was originally known as Diaz, a village in the Rio Grande Valley mostly populated by Mexicans. In 1907 its name was changed in honour of a local rancher, Benjamin Hicks, who was fondly remembered for his saintly charity and good nature. It grew steadily from this point on, and by December 18, 1932, when George and Clara Gibson's twin daughters were born, San Benito was officially a city, though still of modest proportions. Along with their older sister Ann, Doris and Luis Gibson spent the next twelve years of their lives there, before the Gibson family moved to San Antonio in 1945. A year later they moved again, to Denver, before finally settling in Oakwood, California in early 1947.

Doris and Luis were bright, blonde and identically beautiful, and were well aware of the added impact they could make when appearing side by side. They started fashion modelling while still at high school, and both went on to major in Art at the University of Berkley and the California School of Arts and Crafts. They even stuck together in their first jobs after college, both signing on as stewardesses with American Airlines. Because of their bilingual backgrounds they were assigned to the airline's Mexico run, and it was on one of these short hops across the Mexican border, during 1954, that Doris was chatted up by a suave and charming male passenger, who asked her out on a date. Flustered, she asked the pilots for advice, who were unanimous in their recommendations. Unlike Doris, they recognised the passenger as a popular Dallas-area TV star and actor, one Jerome Martin Haynes, better known as Jerry and soon to be even better known to children across America as that avuncular avatar of educational television fun, Mr Peppermint.

Jerry Haynes was born on January 31, 1927 in Dallas. He graduated from Woodrow Wilson High School in 1944 and went on to study at Louisiana State University (for one semester) and Yale (for a year), where his studies in Japanese led Haynes to serve as an information specialist in the US Air Force. Returning to Dallas, he completed his education at Southern Methodist University (SMU), studying Drama alongside future *Charlie's Angels* and *Dynasty* producer Aaron Spelling and *Benson* actor James Noble, before graduating with a BA in Speech and Theatre.

A scholarship from the American Theatre Wing allowed Haynes to travel to New York's Greenwich Village in 1950, to study under Herbert Berghof at his HB Studio, which the legendary acting coach had established at the end of the war. Later alumni would include Liza Minnelli, Al Pacino and Robert De Niro, but Haynes' attempts to establish himself as a serious young actor in the Marlon Brando mould went nowhere, leaving him broke and disillusioned. So in 1952 he once again returned to Dallas, where he began working as a broadcaster on the city's fledgling TV channel WFAA-TV. It was soon after this that Haynes propositioned the attractive blonde stewardess on a flight to Mexico, and he and Doris were married in 1955. Their first child arrived on September 30, 1957: Gibson Jerome Haynes, better known to his friends as Gibby.

It's always been a source of wonder and amusement to journalists and commentators that the seemingly deranged and decadent singer with notoriously obscene psycho-punks the Butthole Surfers should be the son of a well-known children's TV star. Indeed, one could not get more anodyne, all-American or gosh-darned wholesome than Mr Peppermint. But there it is: Gibby, soon joined by a brother, Andrew, and a sister, Clara, enjoyed a happy and prosperous childhood as the son of a local celebrity in a polite Dallas suburb, and seems to have emerged with no deeper psychological scars than something to prove and a certain sense of entitlement.

"It was badass," Gibby recalled, when asked what it was like having a local TV star as a dad. "At the drag races I actually got to go in the pits. We'd get free tickets to Six Flags. In fourth grade I actually got in a fistfight because someone called my dad a clown. That Spanish song 'One Ton Tomato' ['Guantanamera']? We went on vacation in Acapulco and my dad sang that song with Trini Lopez in a bar. He's a player."

At WFAA, Jerry Haynes was initially an enthusiastic all-rounder, happiest as a sports commentator but just as capable broadcasting the news or co-hosting a cookery show as he was presenting Dallas's local equivalent of *American Bandstand*. But he would become best known for the character he created in 1961 to front the network's flagship children's show: Mr Peppermint.

Haynes hosted the hour long *Mr Peppermint Show* every week from 1961 to 1969, dressed in his trademark candy-striped blazer and straw boater (openly lifted from Meredith Willson's musical *The Music Man*) and carrying his magic cane. His puppet sidekicks included Muffin the Bear, Sherbet Dog, Gaylord Lion and Jingles the Dragon, who acted as foils to the always calm and patriarchal Peppermint. Ever educational (sometimes tryingly so), the show took place in a low-budget but colourful pre-psychedelic wonderland, until it was axed at the end of the sixties. This was not the end however, and Mr Peppermint returned in the magazine-format *Peppermint Place* in 1975, which would run for another 21 years.

One of the earliest TV celebrities, Mr Peppermint was also one of the most-loved. Generations of kids responded to his gentle authority and his warm, friendly nature, which was apparently entirely genuine. Unlike some children's entertainers, Haynes loved working with and talking to the very young, and this warmth and empathy extended to his own family. But he also wasn't above enjoying the odd moment of mischievous provocation, such as the time a young boy told him on air that he enjoyed a sip of bourbon with his breakfast. Indeed those early, live-broadcast Mr Peppermint shows were often exercises in barely-controlled chaos, with children and live animals running around and defecating among collapsing scenery and exploding props, and Haynes attempting to stay serene and in charge at the centre of it all. Put that way, it's not such a great leap from Mr Peppermint to the notorious spectacle of his son's band's later performances.

Jerry Haynes was also a decent character actor on stage and screen, though his film work consisted mainly of made-for-TV specials. His second major claim to fame after being Mr Peppermint was as the first to break the news of the Kennedy assassination, appearing on local TV news shortly after the shooting with his program director Jay Watson. The two had been within earshot of the tragedy while taking lunch in Dallas, and rushed eyewitnesses into the nearby studio to tell their story. Haynes then went home to his family, where he gathered his young children together and solemnly broke the news to them of their president's inexplicable murder. One can't help wondering how deeply this affected the young Gibby, as the supposed assassin, Lee Harvey Oswald, was a recurring reference point in his early work.

Gibby helped out on his dad's show in the mid-sixties as one of Mr Peppermint's young 'Gumdrops' (local kids recruited to be the equivalent of Mickey Mouse's Mouseketeers – another gumdrop of note was the young Morgan Fairchild). Here he picked up some useful clowning skills, doing pratfalls from chairs and blowing bubbles within bubbles. It's not hard to see how this pseudo-circus childhood influenced Gibby's future career, giving him a taste for performing and being the centre of attention. The younger Haynes may have gone on to become a poster boy for amorality, chaos and drug-fuelled degradation, but he was always in showbiz, an entertainer first and foremost. Jerry Haynes recognised this and always remained extremely proud of his son's achievements, though with typical knowing playfulness he always insisted on referring to his band as "the Buffalo Surfers".

Throughout his childhood, however, it was a love of sports that seemed to be Gibby's strongest connection to his father. At Lake Highlands Junior High, he set new scoring records as a basketball player and was no slouch on the football field, impressing his peers with the range, velocity and accuracy of his passes. And if Gibby's height and stamina helped him to achieve athletically, then a quick-witted intelligence and insatiable curiosity ensured that he was also top of his class in most academic subjects. In short, the young Gibby Haynes was smart, successful and popular, with a home life that was comfortable, entertaining and, by all accounts, extremely loving and supportive. There was no trace of any trauma or alienation that might explain his future work, despite the darker aspects of his high school experience that Gibby later reflected on in the Buttholes' sole hit single, the blatantly autobiographical 'Pepper.' He did however show signs of a restless creativity, a hunger for new sensations and the bored frustration that smart, imaginative kids are often prone to, even when everything seems to be going their way. That temptation to fuck shit up, just to see what happens, can become too strong to resist.

In most respects though, Gibby remained the perfect student. In 1978 he enrolled at Trinity University in San Antonio on an athletics scholarship, majoring in Accounting and Economics. He became the captain of the college basketball team, president of the Theta fraternity and Trinity's star accountancy student. At the same time, however, he was now also a 6' 4" punk rocker with spiked hair and a leather jacket, at a time when hardly anyone in Texas, let alone San Antonio, was rocking the punk look. Back in the late seventies, San Antonio was very much redneck territory, and no-one wanted the kind of attention that being a first-generation punk would bring. If the freaks and the hippies had it bad in Texas in the sixties, then the punks had it double at least.

"Gibby was one of the first guys on Campus to jump into the whole punk thing," recalled Scott Mathews, who was then majoring in Art at Trinity and was part of a small core of punk fans at the university. That group also included his fellow Art student Paul Leary Walthall, who immediately took a shine to gangly, insouciant punk Haynes. "He had a nice stereo and listened to cool music," Leary says of Gibby. "Gibby turned me on to punk and new wave. We became instant friends."

Born in San Antonio on May 7, 1957, Paul Leary was the son of the Dean of the Business School at Trinity, and it's said that Paul was all set to become a stockbroker after graduation, though he was majoring in Art alongside Business. "I was free to pursue whatever I wanted," Paul says. "My parents would have loved to see me become a professional artist." And though it makes a good story to highlight that future punk rock anarchists Paul and Gibby studied business and accountancy before forming the Butthole Surfers, in fact the band's origins can be firmly traced to the Trinity University Art Department.

"Paul and I were Art majors at Trinity, and Gibby was Paul's best friend who was majoring in Business," Scott Mathews told Austin punk historian Chris Smart in 2001. "Paul used to go around San Antonio writing things on peoples' doors and stuff. He had little Xerox things with little phrases like 'self-contained unit' that he used to paste on peoples' doors. He was into that whole guerrilla art thing."

Leary and Mathews were interested in performance and installation art, and the work of pioneering artists like Yves Klein, Joseph Beuys, the Vienna Actionists and Chris Burden, the Californian artist best known for nailing himself to the roof of a Volkswagen Beetle in a crucifixion pose in April 1974.

Gibby, meanwhile, was developing his surrealist family entertainment values, entering an art contest with a piece called 'Hold The Pickles At Auschwitz' that led to him being hauled up in front of the college authorities for anti-Semitism, and being arrested by the campus police for repeatedly playing tennis in the nude. Soon all three found their imaginations captured by punk rock and the way that it was shaking up the status quo, annoying people who'd never heard of the Fluxus movement or Dadaism – in short, the very people who most needed shaking up and annoying.

Punk in San Antonio and nearby Austin – ninety minutes away on Interstate 35 – had been kicked off by a notorious Sex Pistols concert at Randy's Rodeo in San Antonio on January 8, 1978. This was one of a handful of dates on the Pistols' ill-fated US tour, which consisted of half a dozen shows in small clubs in the southern states, intended to bring punk to the 'real people' rather than the scenesters on either coast. The Pistols also felt that Texans and other southerners would see the humour in the UK punk movement. Like much of the Pistols' activity, this was perceived at the time as a badly-conceived publicity stunt, intended merely to generate conflict and headlines. But with hindsight it seems to have been highly effective; Austin, for instance, would have the earliest and most exciting punk scene in the US outside of New York.

A decade earlier Austin had birthed one of the key pre-punk acts in the form of the incredible 13th Floor Elevators, but the city authorities had done their best to shut them down, along with like-minded acts like the Golden Dawn and a pre-fame Janis Joplin. By the mid-seventies, psychedelia had been and gone, and Austin was known for a scene that fused hippy vibes with country music, the laid-back but fiercely independent 'cosmic cowboy' movement centred on legendary Austin music venue the Armadillo World Headquarters (known colloquially as the 'Dillo). In many ways this represented everything about seventies rock that the Pistols were set on destroying, and some believe the show was booked in San Antonio purely to annoy Austin music snobs. Certainly Randy's Rodeo, an unreconstructed redneck cowboy beer joint, was the most suitably unsuitable venue the much-hyped avatars of punk could have chosen. Nevertheless, over 2,000 people descended upon Randy's Rodeo that night – nearly four times as many as on other dates on the tour. San Antonio already had its own small proto-punk scene brewing, including support act the Vamps, who played mostly Stooges and New York Dolls numbers, and other bands like the Violators and the Skunks.

Just as importantly, however, San Antonio was at that time the number one market for hard rock in the country, made up of a working class mix of Mexicans and Anglos who loved loud, obnoxious heavy metal and embraced punk in the same spirit. They were joined by a frustrated minority of Austin music fans who hated the laid-back cosmic cowboy scene that had taken over their town. Proto-punk legend Iggy Pop had played the Armadillo the year before, drawing a small but intense crowd of 200, and those same fans would recognise each other again at the Pistols' San Antonio date.

In fact, despite Rotten famously taunting the crowd from the stage with "All you cowboys are faggots," the regulars at Randy's stayed away, and the hail of bottles, cans, coins, spittle and cream pies that rained down on the stage came not from cowboys but from long-haired rock kids, eager to kick Rotten's limey ass all the way back to London. There were also journalists from all over the states, UK writers flown in to cover the event, and a whole great posse of cops, Sheriff's deputies and FBI Agents, not to mention Jesus freaks outside the show hollering about sin and damnation. Within a week, the Sex Pistols would implode onstage at San Francisco's Winterland Ballroom, but their impact on Texas (they also played in Dallas a couple of nights later) would last far longer.

"The Sex Pistols left no unfinished business," Margaret Moser would later write in the *Austin Chronicle*. "Those of us in attendance were handed marching orders, effective January ninth, 1978, to rage against mediocrity." Paul Leary was among those in attendance who felt so charged.

Growing up, Leary was a typical San Antonio rock kid who dug Grand Funk Railroad, Creedence Clearwater Revival and Frank Zappa. He had played in several high school garage bands, though the only band name that anyone can recall is the possibly ironic Crowd Pleasers. But although his ears had been opened up to punk rock by the Pistols, Leary had given up playing the guitar by the time he arrived at Trinity, and after graduating in 1980 was working part-time in a lumber yard while starting a master's degree in finance.

"I talked Paul and Gibby into doing something, because the whole punk thing was so strong," Scott Mathews claimed. "Paul had played guitar since he was a little kid. He sort of revealed it one day. Every weekend we were going up to Austin seeing bands because the whole punk thing had exploded. The energy of the Austin scene was overtaking all of us. We were just smoking pot and drinking beer. One day Paul said he played guitar, and I found a set of drums and learned to play."

"Gibby had to really beg me to pick up the guitar again," Paul claims. "But once I did, my days of working at the lumber yard were numbered." Fired up by punk, the new music that Gibby, Paul and Scott set out to make was going to be about ideas rather than technique; a total rejection of the early seventies orthodoxy where Clapton was god and the likes of Alvin Lee were revered for how many notes they could play per second.

"One of the main themes was how horrible music was at the time, and in the late seventies," Gibby would recall, years later. "And then the Ramones, the Dead Kennedys and Circle Jerks started kicking it and they were real noisy, man! You know, growing up to shit like classic rock sucked, and all of a sudden this shit is going on with bands like the Cramps doing traditional music but fucking it up! It was real noisy and it seemed as though it took a lot more imagination than talent to do, and that's what we had. We had imagination. Paul played guitar when he was real young and picked up the guitar again and we started making noise because it was idea based and not musical talent based."

Paul, Gibby and Scott Mathews started jamming together at the tail end of 1980, and in the New Year brought in a friend named Scott Stevens on bass. They were mixing up performance art with music, and their twisted creativity extended into other media too. Most infamous is a zine that Paul and Gibby put together called *Strange VD*, dedicated to documenting fictional diseases and illustrated with the most gruesome genuine medical photographs they could find. The Dead Kennedys' Jello Biafra described it as "the weirdest homemade zine I've seen in my life," and recalled some of the invented ailments covered as including 'pinecone butt' and 'taco leg'.

Meanwhile, Gibby had been named Accounting Student of the Year for 1980 (by Leary's father, in his role as Trinity's Dean of Business), which helped him to land a job as an auditor at Peat, Marwick and Mitchell – at that time the biggest accounting firm in the world. "We'd start practicing and Gibby would come in wearing a suit and tie and strip down to his underwear as he was walking through the door," Leary recalled. "It was a cool little routine." All went well for about a year, until Gibby began surreptitiously printing *Strange VD* on the office photocopier out of hours. Inevitably it wasn't long before he left a photograph of some "wildly mutated" genitalia in the machine; the firm made clear their displeasure, and Gibby handed in his notice not long after.

After the unnamed band had been jamming together for about six months, Scott Mathews scored an art exhibition at the tiny Schon-Davenport Gallery in San Antonio. He decided that for the opening night, on May 17, 1981, his punk group should perform. They got together an eight song set, and went on as the Dick Clark Five (or possibly Dick Smoke; no-one is quite sure).

"It was more of a performance piece than a musical piece," Leary recalled. "It involved lots of stuffed dummies and toasters and Big

Mac hamburgers and things. We played music while Gibby ran around with a piece of meat hanging out of his mouth." Leary occasionally put down his guitar to take over on drums when Scott Mathews decided he wanted to play the saxophone, and Scott Stevens presumably attempted to hold everything together with some rudimentary bass. It's not known whether the band actually played all of the eight numbers they'd got together; the show ended abruptly when gallery owner John Schon pulled the plug halfway through.

Some would consider the show a disaster, but for Gibby and Paul at least it was the birth of a monster. Shock, offence, chaos and noise – all the right ingredients were in place. Although they had not yet adopted the name, the Butthole Surfers had manifested in Texas, and a new demon was loosed upon the earth.

3
WEIRD SHIT

Although they were allowed back to the Schon-Davenport Gallery for a second show to mark the closing of Mathews' exhibition at the end of the month, this amorphous punk-noise-art band didn't immediately become the focus of its members' lives. Gibby graduated from Trinity with honours in the summer of 1981 and he and Leary cut out to LA, where they hung out on Venice Beach and sold t-shirts, bedspreads and pillowcases, all decorated with the image of Lee Harvey Oswald. When this failed to make their fortune, they returned to San Antonio, and only then decided to see if they could make a go of the band – though they still changed their name at virtually every gig.

"We started out as the Dick Clark Five, then we were the Dick Gas Five, then it was the Ashtray Babyheads, then Nine Foot Worm Makes Own Food, Vodka Family Winstons, Abe Lincoln's Bush, Ed Asner's Gay, and The Right To Eat Fred Astaire's Asshole, which was shortened from The Inalienable Right To Eat Fred Astaire's Asshole," recalled Leary, whose musical tastes at this point ran to Black Flag, Circle Jerks, Suicide, Devo, Dead Kennedys and SPK. "Music was an excuse. We had to de-learn how to play."

The regular name changes may also have been because no venue in San Antonio was prepared to knowingly book the band twice. "They hated us there," is how Gibby – who briefly adopted the stage name Dez Moines – summed up their status within the San Antonio music scene. Their line-up, too, remained unstable, and roles were fluid: bassist Scott Stevens would sing nearly as much as Gibby, and Paul would sometimes play drums while Scott Mathews blasted on a plastic saxophone and Gibby thrashed away on guitar. When Scott Stevens left in the fall of 1981 and was replaced by Andrew Mullins, Gibby started playing the sax, which became a staple of the band's act for years to come.

A very rough demo tape made its way to Austin's premier punk band the Big Boys, who liked it enough to offer the group – now calling itself the Bleeding Skulls – regular support slots up in Austin. The Bleeding Skulls name was retained for several shows, partly because in Austin their act was actually appreciated. They even started to gain something of a following, though the band would later claim they had to buy kegs of beer and give out free drinks in order to get anyone to come and see them.

Nevertheless, their demo tape got passed around, and members of the crowd started calling out for the song 'Butthole Surfer' – maybe because they liked it, or maybe just because it was a funny phrase that doubled as an insult. But eventually a local MC confused the song with the band and introduced the group onstage as the Butthole Surfers. It was their first paying gig, and the name was obviously more memorable than Bleeding Skulls, so they decided to stick with it.

"Butthole Manor on Woodlawn was where it all started," Scott Mathews remembered. "I sold my car and bought a 1976 Chevy van so we could haul our shit around Texas. One practice, Gibby ran into my bathroom and came out with a toilet paper roll and sang through it into the mic as an effect. It was the toilet paper roll that led to the bullhorn. I had a sax that I used to play at our early shows and Gibby started playing it later, just sort of squeaking and making noise with it."

After a show in Houston on February 20 1982, Andrew Mullins "lost his marbles" according to Scott Mathews, and quit the band, taking their meagre funds with him. Apparently his plan was to go out into the Mojave Desert and set himself on fire, though he never actually got this together. An early unrecorded Buttholes song, 'Desert' was inspired by this incident, and Mullins was replaced by Scott's brother Quinn on bass, in what many consider the classic early line-up of the band.

"They were doing a lot of TV songs back then," Quinn remembered. "They were doing the theme to *Mannix*, the *Perry Mason* theme. We did the *Brady Bunch* theme in 30 seconds flat. The band was much more 'punk', a hardcore thrash-type band. Gibby took his clothes off a lot onstage, and he was famous for singing through a toilet-paper roll."

It was this line-up that decided to head out to Los Angeles permanently, with the aim of finding a niche and an audience among the booming California hardcore scene. Much as the 13th Floor Elevators and Janis Joplin had done fifteen years earlier, the Butthole Surfers sold all their possessions, piled into a van and headed out west, looking for the Promised Land. And just like their Texan psych forebears, the Butthole Surfers found California much harder going than they expected.

Initially luck seemed to be on their side. Scott Mathews recalled how they met a woman on their first day out there who let them move into her Formosa Avenue house for a month. They also quickly made connections on the local scene, and became friendly with hardcore legends Black Flag. Through the Black Flag connection they recorded a second demo tape with Glen Lockett (AKA Spot), the house producer/engineer at SST Records, the seminal punk-indie label founded by Black Flag's Greg Ginn. This took place in the summer of 1982 at Redondo Beach's Total Access Recording Studios. The resulting tape featured six songs: 'Radical West', 'White, Dumb, Ugly And Poor', 'Something', 'BBQ Pope,' 'I Hate My Job' and 'Matchstick', though Scott Mathews recalled the sessions also possibly including versions of 'Negro Observer' and 'Butthole Surfer'.

Despite this promising start, the band were soon completely penniless and living out of garbage cans, even as they secured occasional gigs with visiting Texan punk bands. Their friends the Big Boys got them on a bill at the Grandia Room in Hollywood that also featured the Minutemen and the Descendants, and MDC (Millions of Dead Cops) offered them a support slot at the Tool And Die club in San Francisco.

The band drove out from LA in their increasingly unreliable van, which broke down as they entered the city. Somehow making it to the venue, with no money and no way to get home, they were told that the gig was cancelled.

Desperate and at the end of their collective tether, the band broke down in tears, until the promoters took pity and let them play a ten minute, three song set. Like in a movie, this turned out to be their big break; the audience included Jello Biafra of the Dead Kennedys, who offered the Buttholes a support slot when the Kennedys played the Whisky a Go Go in Los Angeles on the Fourth of July.

Scott Mathews would later remember the highs rather than the lows. "We played with the Minutemen at the Grandia Room and word got around about us really quickly," he said. "We went up to SF and played this gig and Jello Biafra saw us and freaked out. A week later Jello had us open for the DK and TSOL at the Whisky. It was one of the best things we ever did."

Gibby stripped down to his boxer shorts, sang through the toilet roll tube and threw bags of paper cockroaches into the audience, having got into 'roach art' in San Antonio because there were just so many of them in everyone's apartments. "We'd take clothes and stuff them with cheeseburgers and mousetraps and condoms and tear them apart at shows and throw them at the crowd," Scott Mathews recalled. "We played like two or three encores, and they were still yelling at us when the DKs came on stage. That's when we knew we were, like, a national band – everybody in LA was talking about us the next day."

The band's set already included such future Buttholes classics as 'Negro Observer,' 'Something' 'Bar-b-Q Pope' and their title song, alongside numbers like 'Radical Western World,' 'Matchstick' and 'White, Dumb, Ugly And Poor.' But despite their growing notoriety and Biafra's support, life in LA without money soon proved too much even for the Butthole Surfers, and after about two months they returned to San Antonio, where things became increasingly tense.

"We came back to Texas because it was cheaper to live there and we were starting to fight," Scott Mathews said, adding that despite their success, he was considering quitting the band at that point to become a writer. Gibby's memories, speaking to *Forced Exposure* magazine in 1986, were even less rose-tinted. "Everybody hated us, so we went back to Texas," he said. "We scattered and ran with our legs between our tails."

"Then we realised we couldn't get jobs," Paul Leary added. "Our lives were already ruined."

They played a few more shows around Texas before supporting the Dead Kennedys once more, at the Studio D Club in Dallas, on August 6, 1982. But this would prove to be the Mathews brothers' last stand. "Paul and Gibby took all the money and went to Gibby's dad's house," Scott Mathews later claimed. "They didn't want to pay me and Quinn, so I got in a fist fight with Gibby in Mr Peppermint's front yard in the middle of the night." Other accounts say that Gibby smacked Scott Mathews in the face so hard that he broke his hand.

Scott and Quinn Mathews quit for good, but fate was still covering the Buttholes' ass in the shape of the opening act for the Dallas show, Fort Worth's infamous teen punk band the Hugh Beaumont Experience. Their drummer, Jeffrey King Coffey, found a common ground with Gibby and Paul that included not just punk rock and noise music, but also art and psychedelic drugs.

Coffey and the other members of the Hugh Beaumont Experience were already fans of the Butthole Surfers, having travelled from Fort Worth to Austin in 1982 to check out the already notorious band at the city's Ritz club. "We went down to Austin and saw this band with the lead singer in underwear and clothes pins in his hair," Coffey later recalled. "We tried to recognize the song they were playing, and finally my friend punched me when we realized they were playing 'D.O.A.' [by seventies hard rock band Bloodrock, from Fort Worth, TX] the most uncool song in the world for a hardcore punk rock band to be playing."

The Hugh Beaumont Experience had been formed as the Offenders in 1980 by Sex Pistols obsessed schoolboys Brad Stiles (vocals), Tommie Duncan (guitar), Clay Carlisle (bass) and Carter Kolba (drums), before they settled on their vastly improved name. Hugh Beaumont was the actor who had portrayed the quintessential American TV patriarch Ward Cleaver in classic US sitcom *Leave It To Beaver*, though the name 'The Hugh Beaumont Experience' was actually stolen from a fictional band in a one-panel *Creem* magazine cartoon.* The members of the real band were all pupils at Fort Worth's fee-paying Country Day School, but it should be noted that Clay and Carter were the only real rich kids in the line-up; Brad was on a scholarship, and Tommie's parents, by all accounts, struggled to put him through school. The band practised in their lunch breaks, gigged whenever they could, and were all still aged 15 to 17 when they released their only single, 1981's legendary *Cone Johnson* EP, on local label Cygnus Records.

Brief, basic and bristling, the Beaumonts' loyalty to the early London punk sound is demonstrated on cuts like the one-minute-twenty-one 'Where'd Ya Go Sid,' lamenting that punk rock seemed to have lost all of its *je ne sais quoi* and *joi de vivre* following the titular Mr Vicious's untimely demise. Brad sings in a sneering fake cockney accent throughout, distinguishing the primitivist snot-rock classics 'Zyklon B' and 'Money Means So Much To Me' to the point where the Texan schoolboy's archly elongated vowels almost suggest he's trying out for the part of the Artful Dodger in a local production of *Oliver!*

Nevertheless, for all its debts, the four-song seven-inch was still the first – perhaps the only – punk record to come out of Fort Worth, and when the rich kid rhythm section quit shortly after its release, King Coffey jumped at the chance to audition. A 15-year-old punk and publisher of local fanzine *Throbbing Cattle*, Coffey barely knew how to play the drum kit his beatnik dad had loaned him the deposit for (to stop him destroying all the books and furniture in the house with his drum sticks). But, as he'd anticipated, this wasn't a problem. Perhaps encouraged by the fact that he had almost the same alliterative initials as his predecessor, the Hugh Beaumont Experience welcomed King Coffey with open arms.

With Coffey behind the kit, the Experience started playing more widely, supporting bands like MDC and Dallas heroes Stick Men With Rayguns. By 1982 Tommie Duncan had quit, replaced on guitar by David McCreath, while bassist Clay had been swapped out for another Tommy. Their songs became faster and less structured as the

---

* In his portrayal of Ward Cleaver, Hugh Beaumont has also been noted for his resemblance to JR "Bob" Dobbs, the 'World Avatar' of the Church of the Subgenius, founded by the Reverend Ivan Stang and Philo Drummond in the Fort Worth/Dallas area in 1979.

band discovered the Dicks, Black Flag and Minor Threat and soon found themselves absorbed into the hardcore scene. Somewhere along the line Coffey lost his bass drum pedal, and through necessity adopted the stand-up, Moe Tucker (of the Velvet Underground) style of drumming he would later become known for in the Butthole Surfers.

The band got stranger after Brad discovered acid and persuaded Coffey to start tripping with him. Their hardcore seven inches all sounded dreadful on LSD, so they started listening to old sixties hard rock and psych records. This led to Brad and the band growing their hair, wearing tie dye on stage and doing their best to piss off the hardcore punks by "trying to be the most psychedelic band in the world." At the same time, they were all massively into heavy funk music – Parliament, Cameo, Zapp – and Washington DC's nascent Go-Go sound. In light of such developments, the Hugh Beaumont Experience couldn't help but become increasingly experimental.

Alongside the acid, Brad Stiles had got addicted to Demerol at sixteen and also, according to Coffey, once bought 200 doses of Vicks Sinex Nasal Spray on a dodgy cheque, which he and his boyfriend melted down to make "the worst bathroom crank ever – it burned my nostrils so much, I can't imagine any high being worth that pain." The store owner was naturally suspicious of these punk kids buying 200 Vicks on a cheque and made a note of their car license plate number. When the cheque bounced, he called the cops.

The car happened to belong to bassist Tommy's dad, and he tipped off his son in time for the whole band, minus King, to flee to LA and lie low for a few years. This was literally hours after the Hugh Beaumont Experience had made their final recordings at San Antonio's BOSS Studios in 1983: 'Alchemy,' influenced by the then-current sound of Public Image Limited and Killing Joke, and a more or less faithful cover of Cream's 'Sunshine of Your Love' that had become a staple of their acid-era live set.

Brad Stiles later returned to Austin and formed the short-lived noise band A Child's Garden of Sodom, but was found dead, hung in his closet, in 1993. Tommie Duncan became a teacher in Thailand, while David McCreath became the web co-ordinator for the Anchorage School District in Alaska. And in 1983, King Coffey walked in, barefoot, on the Butthole Surfers, midway through the recording of their first EP, and became their new permanent drummer.

Jello Biafra had told the band that if they recorded an EP's worth of material, he would release it on his Alternative Tentacles record label and reimburse their costs. The only trouble was, at this point there was no band; the Mathews brothers had quit, leaving just Gibby and Paul. They managed to recruit a new bass player, a local musician and jazz fan named Bill Jolly, and enrolled the help of their friends in San Antonio punk band the Marching Plague to guide them through the process of making a record.

The Marching Plague were as close as the Butthole Surfers got to kindred spirits in San Antonio, and were slightly more experienced at recording. The Buttholes borrowed studio time from Bob O'Neill at the aforementioned BOSS (AKA, Bob O'Neill Sound Studio). "It was a demo kind of studio," Leary recalls. "They'd let us record there when nothing else was booked. Gibby and I spent a lot of time hanging out in the tool shed at the back. Our first engineer was a guy who was in a band called Toby Beau; we had, I think, one day to record and mix our first EP, and the engineer spent the first half of the day reading the instructions manual to the Trident board, since he had never actually engineered anything before."

However, Leary's assertion that the band's debut EP was recorded in an afternoon hardly fits with the fact that at least three drummers played on the sessions, or that documented rehearsal and demo recordings for the songs exist, as well as unreleased outtakes. Marching Plague drummer Brad Perkins plays on three songs, as well as on several tracks that were never used for the record; King Coffey apparently turned up two-thirds of the way through the sessions, in time to play on 'Bar-B-Q Pope' and 'Wichita Cathedral.' 'Hey' features studio session drummer Gene Delibero, while Bill Jolly's roommate from UT, Kevin Leman, plays on 'Suicide', and was actually the band's full-time drummer for a short period. Bill Jolly plays bass throughout, except for on 'Wichita Cathedral' where Paul Leary doubles up on bass and guitar. It should also be noted that, while "Trombone Taylor" is credited as producer on the record's sleeve, this was the band's nickname for Bob O'Neill's house engineer (and former Zakary Thaks songwriter) Mike Taylor, a quite distinct character from the mysterious "guy from Toby Beau."*

The seven-song, twelve-inch EP was duly released by Alternative Tentacles in July 1983. Untitled, or eponymously titled, Alternative Tentacles at some point decided to name it *Brown Reasons To Live*, after a phrase originally etched into the vinyl run-out groove, and later represses included this title on the sleeve and spine. The EP is also sometimes known as *Pee Pee The Sailor*, a phrase found on the record's centre label, alongside a crude cartoon of a bum-faced Popeye character.

The record opens with a squeal of feedback, and then a bellowed pronouncement, courtesy of Paul Leary: "There's a time to fuck and a time to pray, but the Shah sleeps in Lee Harvey's grave!" An explosion of thrashing guitars, frenzied drum rolls and moaning, howling voices follows, then stops just as suddenly, before another, equally significant toast is called. "There's a time to shit and a time for God; the last shit I took was pretty fucking odd!" precedes another eruption of hardcore noise, and this cycle continues throughout the song.

'The Shah Sleeps In Lee Harvey's Grave' refers, of course, to Lee Harvey Oswald (supposed Kennedy killer, Texas's least favourite son and, as we've seen, something of an obsession for the young Gibby Haynes) and the last Shah of Iran, Mohammad Reza Pahlavi, who was overthrown by the Ayatollah Khomeini in the 1979 Iranian Revolution. In the 1950s, the Shah had supported a CIA coup to overthrow the Iranian government after it voted to nationalise the country's oil industry, and his continued resistance to communism in the Middle East ensured maintained US support, even as his reign became increasingly dictatorial. By the mid-seventies, he had declared Iran a one-party state, but his moves to steadily increase oil prices gradually chipped away at that crucial American backing, until, at the beginning of 1979, a sudden popular uprising forced him into exile.

---

* Toby Beau were a middle-of-the-road country pop band from South Texas who hit number 1 on the US Easy Listening Chart in 1978 with 'My Angel Baby.' The original line-up consisted of Balde Silva, Danny McKenna, Art Mendoza, Steve Zipper and Rob Young. They moved to San Antonio prior to signing a deal with RCA, at which point Mendoza was replaced by Ron Rose.

It was during this exile that the Shah was allowed to enter the US for emergency medical treatment – he was suffering from gallstones – at the medical centre at Lackland Air Force Base, in the Butthole Surfers' hometown of San Antonio. Surgical complications meant that the Shah's stay extended for six weeks, during which time the new Iranian government furiously demanded his return. Some think this anger at America's continued support for the Shah, even after he had been deposed, led directly to the Iran Hostage Crisis – which, in turn, led to Democrat Jimmy Carter losing the Presidency to Republican Ronald Reagan in the 1980 elections.

Following his death in Egypt on July 27 1980, the Shah was interred in the Al-Rifa'i Mosque in Cairo. Lee Harvey Oswald, meanwhile, was buried in Shannon Rose Hill Memorial Park in Fort Worth. But conspiracy theories persisted that a look-a-like Russian agent had been buried in Oswald's place, and this paranoid whispers built to such a peak during the late seventies that, on October 4 1981, Oswald's body was exhumed so that forensic evidence could finally settle the case once and for all.

Both of these stories – the Shah being treated at a military base in San Antonio, and the rumours that someone else occupied Lee Harvey Oswald's grave – would have been current during Gibby and Leary's student years, which doubled as the Butthole Surfers' early songwriting period. The song probably arose from long nights of stoned bullshitting about conspiracy theories. However it's worth noting that, in the song, the Shah isn't buried in Lee Harvey's grave – he only sleeps there. This is more similar to the idea that the Shah is standing in Lee Harvey's shoes, or that they have common ground in the cyclical nature of history. Certainly, the Shah could be said to have unwittingly precipitated the transition from the liberal President Carter to the conservative President Reagan, just as Oswald unwittingly allowed Lyndon B Johnson to succeed Kennedy. Both were also arguably CIA stooges, who were thrown to the wolves when they had outlived their usefulness.

Beyond this, though, the song functions as a kind of Satanic invocation, calling on all the sacred spirits of rock music and American trash culture in order to transform the Butthole Surfers – an inept Texan punk band – into a demonic force capable of achieving fame, success, glory, and unparalleled feats of excess and destruction. This is the point where the Butthole Surfers gladly offer up their souls for rock'n'roll. "There's a time for drugs and a time to be sane, but Jimi Hendrix makes love to Marilyn's remains," Leary howls, later. "I smoke Elvis Presley's toenails when I want to get high."

Hendrix, Presley, Marilyn Monroe – the Surfers were re-animating these deposed deities of the discredited sixties with their youthful punk energy, while at the same time using them as totems of the fame, success and excess that they hoped to achieve themselves. The thrash interludes sound like some ultra-primitive, orgiastic tribal ritual, and it's tempting to believe that's exactly what they are. Indeed, by the song's end, the ceremony seems to have worked – the very spirit of Rock has manifested, voiced by Marching Plague singer Keith Rumbo. "I am the ultimate God," he proclaims. "Don't even look upon me with your naked eyes," while another voice hopelessly whimpers "Shut up!" over and over, as though driven half mad by what he has seen emerging from the smoke and devastation.

By contrast, 'Hey' is almost folky; resembling the contemporary tribal goth-rock of UK bands Skeletal Family or Sex Gang Children in its driving one-note bassline, quivering vocal effects and descending minor key, chorus-pedal-coated guitar arpeggios. Leary kicks in with a sweet distorted solo as the song shifts up a gear, while Gibby half chants, "I'm not fit to fall in love," repeating the word "love" as a question, as though the very concept were alien to him.

Continuing to move through genres, 'Something' is a distorted take on early-eighties hip-hop, with Paul Leary screech-rapping over a sluggish groove similar to the Sugarhill Gang's 'Rapper's Delight' (1979) or Queen's 'Another One Bites the Dust' (1980)* – both of which were based upon Chic's 1979 classic 'Good Times'. Guitars even imitate the sound of scratching, as fuzz bass and sax lay down an ominous groundswell. Leary almost seems to be spontaneously free-associating, and contributes some warped slide guitar as the rhythm section lock into some tight if basic funk.

---

* 'Another One Bites the Dust' was the centre of a controversy over "backwards masking", after it was alleged that the song's chorus, played backwards, sounded like "It's fun to smoke marijuana." Though the band and their record company denied this, it's the sort of stunt the Butthole Surfers would have approved of.

'Bar-B-Q Pope' returns to the descending, minor-key goth-folk guitars of 'Hey', over which Leary continues screeching like a demented parakeet, alternating with blurts of saxophone from Gibby. "They shot the pope! They shot the Pope's ass!" If the EP can be seen as some kind of musical black mass, then this symbolic sacrifice and defiling of the head of the Catholic Church must be a necessary ingredient. And who is "I-Calypso", introduced at the beginning of the song and returning in the whispered, spoken mid-section? The phrase has echoes of both "apocalypse" and "I Collapse", while also sounding like the name of some strange voodoo spirit. Calypso, of course, was the Greek Nymph who held Odysseus hostage on her island for seven years. James Joyce also took her name for a chapter in *Ulysses,* and one can easily imagine the notion of shooting and barbecuing the pope in a dream coming from Joyce's classic novel of the Irish collective unconsciousness.

'Wichita Cathedral' comes close to the Birthday Party's blazing, psychotic goth-rockabilly, but never accelerates much above crooning pace. 'Suicide' is a faster punk thrash, but seems throwaway, paradoxically because it sounds like it's earnestly trying to say something serious: "I've got a stiff upper lip because I'm half dead." "I'm not fucking kidding, man, it hurts," the song ends plaintively. But rock n' roll has no sympathy – a creepy, slowed-down cry of "Your pain makes me hungry – I'm hungry for pain," is the immediate response, leading into 'The Revenge of Anus Presley'.

If the EP's first song was in fact some kind of All-American Satanic ritual, then its final track represents the ultimate result. The demonic spirit of rock returns, emerging from the smoke and devastation: Anus Presley himself, the concentrated fatty essence of deep-fried southern rock'n'roll, let loose upon our putrid Earth like some silver-sequined, jumpsuited, be-sideburned Godzilla, trampling the band underfoot in the studio. "Your life is mine!" it roars, over squalling free-noise guitars and dragging drums, voiced once more by Keith Rumbo. "Revenge is mine! You're the one that's gonna pay this time, buddy..."

The music is the sound of panic, of a band attempting to flee but realising it is too late: they are trapped, with a monster of their own making, one that will surely devour them. The song is oddly prophetic; the Butthole Surfers had indeed given their lives to rock'n'roll, and during the ensuing years they would pay for it many times over.

4

FREAK PARTY

Upon its initial release in July 1983, the Butthole Surfers' debut EP was notable for the complete lack of information displayed on its sleeve. There were no credits for who had played on the record; there weren't even any song titles, although this was rectified when Alternative Tentacles repressed the record as *Brown Reasons To Live*. Initially however, the record simply boasted the band's name and a sticker boasting "free single!" This turned out to be a seven-inch by a completely unrelated band named Voice Farm, courtesy of distributors Subterranean. Maybe this was a desperate attempt to sell this record by a completely unknown group who had nothing going for them but a comically obscene moniker and a lot of mystique. Maybe too much mystique, as Spinal Tap could've said.

The Buttholes continued to play live around Texas through the first half of 1983, with Gibby, Paul and Bill Jolly joined by Kevin Leman on drums for a handful of shows. A long-haired guy who one suspects never fully took to punk rock, never mind hardcore, Leman finally quit after a rowdy concert at Studio 29 on February 4, when a bottle thrown at Gibby from the crowd ended up hitting the hapless drummer full in the face. From then on, Marching Plague drummer Brad Perkins would fill in whenever his commitment to his main band allowed, until King Coffey finally joined in June.

Following the EP's release, the Butthole Surfers relocated to Austin, where they rented a rehearsal space in a downtown warehouse for forty dollars a month from a local performance artist and musician named Teresa Taylor. A Radio, Film and Television major at the University of Texas in Austin, Taylor played drums in a similar stand-up style to Coffey. The band had only played about three shows with Coffey on drums, but already they had started thinking about bringing in a second drummer to strengthen the rhythmic, hypnotic backbone that anchored the chaos and noise onstage. Teresa joined them for a few rehearsal/jam sessions, and the results were spectacular enough for them to offer her the gig permanently.

The petite, androgynous-looking Taylor may have seemed an unlikely candidate for joining a band that was so stinkily, scatologically male, especially when the members – and their members – were constantly forced into scarily intimate confines with each other. But Taylor soon proved a kindred spirit to Gibby, Leary and Coffey, with a shared love of conceptual art and ferocious punk rock. And she was far tougher than she looked, with the discipline and stamina to stand alongside Coffey pounding out the same heavy, tribal beat for hours on end. Rechristened Teresa Nervosa, she would stand side by side with King Coffey on stage, both of them maintaining a driving, hypnotic rhythm as the chaos raged around them. They looked similar enough to pass for brother and sister, and claimed as much to journalists for years, saying that they had previously played in their high school marching band together.

The Surfers continued recording on credit at BOSS, amassing enough material for a full album. The problem was, Alternative Tentacles weren't coming forward with the money to pay for the sessions. As a stopgap while the label got over its cash flow problems, they agreed to release a live EP, recorded by Mike Taylor at the Meridian Club in San Antonio on March 25 1984, and mixed and assembled by Taylor at BOSS. *Live PCPPEP* came out on Alternative Tentacles in September, and featured live versions of five of the seven tracks from their debut EP, plus opener 'Cowboy Bob' and the thirty-four second 'Dance Of The Cobras' (actually a sped-up version of 'Woly Boly').

Both the band and the studio were growing increasingly impatient with Alternative Tentacles, however. The label still hadn't taken up their option on the Butthole Surfers' debut album and, more importantly, neither had they paid the band's studio bills. "I remember calling Alternative Tentacles about a year after our first record had come out," Leary said. "I asked if we were going to get paid for the records they sold, and their response was, 'We need the money to finance the next Dead Kennedys album.' The honeymoon ended there."

Bob O'Neill eventually decided that the only way that he was going to get his money back would be if he released the album on his own Ward 9 label. The only previous release on Ward 9 had been the seminal Texan hardcore anthology *Cottage Cheese From The Lips of Death* (1983), compiled by Gibby and including the Butthole Surfers track 'I Hate My Job' alongside other songs recorded at BOSS from the Dicks, Big Boys, Really Red, Stickmen With Rayguns and the Hugh Beaumont Experience, among others. Gibby even provided the cover art for this release – characteristically childlike, gory and sexually explicit all at the same time.

Despite this, the band had no intention of being railroaded into releasing their debut LP through Ward 9. With Alternative Tentacles dragging their feet, they began looking for another label who could buy out the master tapes from O'Neill. It was at this point that Touch And Go Records called and asked if the Buttholes were interested in putting out a record with them.

Founded in 1981, the Michigan-based indie label had grown out of a hardcore punk zine of the same name, published by a couple of kids named Dave Stimson and Tesco Vee. By 1983, however, the label was being run by nineteen-year-old Corey Rusk and his girlfriend, Lisa Pfahler. Rusk had been the bassist for hardcore band the Necros, whose *Sex Drive* EP had been Touch And Go's first release, though Rusk had yet to join the band when the EP was recorded. He left two years later to concentrate on running the rapidly growing label, after Tesco Vee moved from Lansing, Michigan to concentrate on his own punk band, the Meatmen.

Rusk had been a fan of the Buttholes since hearing their first demo tape, which had been widely circulated in second and third generation copies among the US punk underground. He'd been trying to contact them for some time, but this was hard work in the days before internet and mobile phones, especially with the scattered and nomadic lives the Butthole Surfers were leading back then. Remember what we said about too much mystique? Eventually, though, Rusk tracked the band down, and arranged to meet them.

Rusk and Pfahler organised a showcase gig for the band at the Paycheck Lounge in Hamtramck, Michigan on August 11 1984, and invited them to stay over at their Detroit apartment. The various band members by this point were drifting between Austin and San Antonio, with Gibby and Leary working as dishwashers and both still effectively homeless. They were itching to get out of Texas, and this was the spur for them to once again sell up and hit the road; in their minds the Michigan show was the first stop of a yet-to-be-organised endless tour.

Meanwhile, Bill Jolly had left the Surfers in June of '84, for unknown reasons; Paul Leary later claimed that he had "forgotten he was in the band." On the first of July they played at the Woodshock Festival, held on a ranch at Dripping Springs, Texas, with former Hugh Beaumont Experience member David McCreath helping out on bass. However, bootlegs of this show reveal the usual chaos and instrument-swapping onstage, with Bill Jolly actually returning to play a bass solo on the final number, even though he had already quit.

Jolly's full-time replacement was Terence Smart, whose Chevy Nova would be customised and brutalised to become the Butthole Surfers' new touring vehicle. They also had one other new member: a pretty, placid pit bull terrier bitch that Paul Leary had rescued from the San Antonio pound, and had named Mark Farner of Grand Funk Railroad, after the singer of his favourite seventies rock band. She was actually the band's second dog; the first, just named "brown dog" was hit by a car and killed during the Buttholes' first San Francisco stay.

With 'Ladykiller' scrawled down the side and '69' painted on the hood, barbed wire attached to the front bumper, shark's teeth painted on the grill, the back seat removed to allow the band members to all lie down together like sardines (their guitars, amps, strobe lights and two drum kits were all packed into a U-haul trailer), Smart's car was deemed roadworthy, and like some post-apocalyptic gypsy tribe or Satanic cult family, the Buttholes went out to look for America.

"I was 22 years old when I joined the band," Teresa later recalled. "We travelled three years straight. We never came back to Austin. We literally did the whole country that way for three years."

The Michigan showcase went well; Rusk and Pfahler thought the Buttholes were the most amazing live band they'd seen, and hit it off with them personally as well. Touch And Go agreed to put out their album, and to split profits on a fifty-fifty basis. There was never any written contract, merely a handshake deal, which was Touch And Go's standard way of dealing with bands, thus avoiding expensive lawyers. It was considered the ethical indie way, a gentleman's agreement, but it would come back to haunt both parties in years to come.

Psychic... Powerless... Another Man's Sac was released by Touch And Go in December 1984, with initial pressings on clear vinyl. The eleven tracks all still featured Bill Jolly on bass, even though he was no longer in the band by the time of the LP's release, and Mike 'Trombone' Taylor at BOSS was still the de facto producer. "Bob O'Neill started engineering our next project," Paul Leary remembers, referring to *Psychic...*, "But he didn't want to spend that much time with us. Trombone was willing to work for cheap, and seemed to like the music, so he ended up doing a lot of the engineering. I learned to do some myself for those nights Bob would let us spend the night in the studio by ourselves."

Although it was ultimately released on Touch And Go, the album definitely sounds as though it was recorded with Alternative Tentacles in mind. Several songs ape the high-tension, surf-gothic hardcore punk of the Dead Kennedys, while Gibby sings in a gulping, bleating style not altogether removed from that of Jello Biafra. This being the Buttholes, it's hard to tell whether they were parodying their new paymasters or simply trying to fit in at the new workplace. Released on Touch And Go however, the album's joke – if that's what it was – went largely unnoticed.

The album opens with 'Concubine', a noise-metal jam with distorted, unhinged vocals, possibly about the kind of weird groupies who would be attracted to a band like the Butthole Surfers. 'Eye of the Chicken' sounds like early eighties electro-pop gone horribly wrong, its clean, propulsive bass and drum chassis thrown into chaos by phased, overdriven guitar squeals and hideous vocoder abuse. 'Dum Dum' is partly based upon 'Children Of The Grave' from Black Sabbath's *Master Of Reality* LP, but in its lo-fi, amateurish arrangement sounds more like the tribal, positive-punk, goth stomp of Sex Gang Children or Southern Death Cult, as well as the Dead Kennedys. Gibby's lyrics seem to be about the absurdity of human relationships and interactions, riffing off King and Teresa's powerful rolling drum patterns.

'Woly Boly' is another of the band's psychobilly chicken-dancing numbers, but more powerful and successful than the earlier 'Wichita Cathedral' in assimilating the sound of the Cramps or the Birthday Party and dragging it back to Captain Beefheart territory. Leary's twisted guitar part is certainly worthy of either Roland S Howard or Zoot Horn Rollo. 'Negro Observer' is a complete change of pace, the clean, jangly guitar and minimal bass and drums almost suggesting Young Marble Giants or the Passions' first album, while the saxophone takes us on a weird sideways trip to 'Echo Beach'. Gibby is still singing in a Jello Biafra bleat, though what's most striking is how uncertain and vulnerable he sounds when not using vocal effects, his voice cracking and frequently floundering off key. It's endearing, yet at this early stage Gibby is obviously still uncomfortable as a singer, still looking for ways to disguise his voice or to avoid singing at all, delegating vocal chores and playing saxophone instead.

What he is singing here is a cryptic, paranoid sci-fi fantasy mixing up Philip K Dick, 1950s Cold War movies like *Invasion Of The Body Snatchers*, and Robert Calvert-era Hawkwind. "Landing in the parking lots in deserted discount stores, Negro Observers are landing by the scores," Gibby warbles. "Dropping down in low rider cars… counting heads in singles bars." Surreal and unsettling, this would become one of the band's best-loved numbers. Side one ends with the song 'Butthole Surfer', a clanging surf-punk crowd-pleaser, rooted in sixties garage as filtered through eighties hardcore, and once again with more than a whiff of the Dead Kennedys or comedy frat-punks like the Dickies.

Side two opens with the redneck cowboy fuzz-stomp of 'Lady Sniff', a love song of sorts suited to many contemporary American working class households, interrupted by frequent farts, belches and spittoon-filling expectorations. It's followed by the astonishing 'Cherub', the first overtly psychedelic song of the Buttholes' career: a spiralling abyss of bass and tremolo driven space rock with distorted spoken vocals, seemingly concerning a demon that's mistaken for an angel. The song builds to a nightmarish climax of squealing, claustrophobic walls of guitar and cruelly mocking vocals, as the deluded protagonist dies a lonely and meaningless death.

'Mexican Caravan' is a more extreme, fractured take on the Damned's 'Neat Neat Neat' or, again, the Dead Kennedys' 'Holiday in Cambodia', but with lyrics about scoring smack south of the border. Leary takes lead vocals.

'Cowboy Bob' kicks in like Hawkwind's 'Brainstorm', with Lemmy-esque bass and sax blurts worthy of Nik Turner, all flanged vocals and headbanging downer psychedelia. Finally, 'Gary Floyd', named after the singer with Texan punk legends the Dicks, is like a sixties garage punk take on folk rock, recalling the Leaves' version of 'Hey Joe' both in its jangling guitar chords and theme of reckless gunplay. Leary once again sings lead, and turns in a classic garage-psych guitar solo.

Still rooted in hardcore punk but pulling towards something weirder, more deranged and interesting, *Psychic... Powerless... Another Man's Sac* is a joyously incompetent, freaky party record. Many still regard it as the band's finest moment, but in truth the Butthole Surfers are still finding their feet, not to mention their balls. As the title perhaps unconsciously suggests, it's still too derivative, and its undeniable energy really belongs to other acts. Much of the fun of the record is hearing how the Buttholes fail to achieve the sound they're aiming for, and through their deficiencies actually create something wilder and stranger, 'Cherub' being the strongest example of this. *Psychic...* is still a really good punk record. But happily, future Butthole Surfers releases would proceed in the direction of sounding less like any generic precedent, and more and more like their fucked-up selves.

For the next couple of years the band essentially lived hand to mouth, travelling across the country on haphazardly organised tours (random one-night stands booked personally by Gibby), and staying at assorted temporary crash pads for nights or weeks at a time between shows. As often as not, they stayed with Corey and Lisa in Detroit, and the band would often rely upon the label to bail them out when their van was confiscated by the police, or they needed money to go into the studio. Through August and September of 1984 they were largely based in New York, using the East Village apartment of scenester and Touch And Go employee Terry Tolkin as a crash pad and surviving like hobos, gathering empty cans and bottles on the streets of New York and turning them in to collect the deposit.

Physically wretched and completely impoverished, any money they did make went back into the band – replacing Smart's ruined Nova with a second-hand van (which turned out to be an unreliable, gas-guzzling liability), or buying several thousand dollars' worth of stolen strobe lights at a tenth of the price. They also added film projections to their arsenal, which became an essential part of their live show. As an RFT major, Teresa had access to a small library of 16mm films, from which the band chose the sickest and most graphic footage, depicting farming accidents and, most notoriously, penile reconstruction surgery, which the band intercut with innocuous cartoon clips and episodes of *Charlie's Angels*. Soon the University of Texas was receiving regular requests from a Dr Haynes for films of extreme medical procedures. As the band's notoriety spread, they also started receiving sick videotapes from fans in the mail, which were gleefully put to use.

Butthole Surfers shows were now nightmarish multi-media extravaganzas. You no longer needed to take acid at their shows, and if you did, chances were you'd be pushed all the way over the edge by their performance. When the Buttholes added smoke machines to their sensory arsenal, the films refused to stay safely on the back wall, instead surging forward into the audience on clouds of dry ice in a kind of primitively effective 3D. Coffey and Nervosa's double drumming thundered in time to the strobes set up under their snares, while Gibby, now barking through a bullhorn rather than a simple toilet roll tube, set fire to a cymbal doused in lighter fluid, sending a geyser of flame spurting joyfully towards the ceiling each time he hit it.

Gibby might take to the stage with a life-size mannequin taped to his body, which he would then proceed to destroy. Or he would fill his clothes with fake blood capsules that would burst open gorily as he hurled himself around the stage. On other occasions, the whole band would tear a collection of cute stuffed animals to shreds during their performance. The theatrics were cheap, simple and ingenious, but incredibly effective, especially to a post-punk audience used to seeing crop-haired men in black t-shirts playing their songs with a puritanical disregard for spectacle. By comparison, the Butthole Surfers seemed like a Cecil B DeMille apocalypse.

In January 1985 the band decided, while tripping, that they should move to Athens, Georgia and stalk REM, who had just broken out of the indie scene and begun to achieve mainstream success with their melodic, ambiguous fusion of arty post-punk and sixties folk-rock. They actually managed to get a house together in the nearby village of Winterville, and worked through their obsession with the increasingly popular and unchallenging local combo, who steadfastly refused the Buttholes' earnest entreaties to come party with them after buttonholing various members in clubs or supermarket aisles. A plan to park the band's van in Michael Stipe's driveway, emblazoned with the legend "Michael Stipe, despite the hype, I still wanna suck your big long pipe" was abandoned, but a couple of years later the Butthole Surfers did add REM's breakthrough hit 'The One I Love' to their sets, ritually desecrating and disembowelling the song at the close of a night's entertainment. Another attraction of life in Athens was that, in nearby Atlanta, the band had a fan base of artists and drag queens who frequented the city's Celebrity Club, including a pre-fame RuPaul, and Kathleen Lynch, who the band would meet again in New York the following year.

Once again though, it was the bassist who cracked first. Unable to stand the gruelling poverty, discomfort and malnutrition being in the Buttholes entailed, Terence Smart quit after a show in Atlanta on January 25 1985. "I guess I'd had enough by then," Smart later recalled. "I was emaciated and sick; I'd had diarrhoea for two weeks straight, I mean real bad diarrhoea. I remember the show there because I had to leave the stage to go sit on the toilet, and then return to finish the show." Smart also had no desire to move to Athens, and so returned home to Texas alone.

Touch And Go found the band a replacement in the shape of Canadian high school tuba player Trevor Malcolm, whose stolen high school tuba came with him. Malcolm lasted about six months then also quit suddenly, and the band recruited their Athens weed dealer, Juan Molina, to help out on a series of US dates in the summer of 1985. Molina actually turned out to be a pretty good bass player, but he wasn't interested in joining the band full time, and was unable to accompany them on their first European tour. He was replaced by Mark Kramer, whose cult New York band Shockabilly had just broken up. He had yet to found the legendary Shimmy Disc Records and the equally cultish Bongwater.

Kramer was already a friend and a fan of the band, and Shockabilly had been reasonably successful in Europe, playing there many times, so he knew the ropes – unlike the Buttholes, who had never been out of the States before. Unfortunately, this also meant that many promoters considered the Butthole Surfers to be simply "Kramer's new band," and even sometimes billed them as Shockabilly, or ex-Shockabilly. This led to some riotous gigs where the audience responded violently to getting a very different band than the one they expected. Needless to say, the Butthole Surfers gave as good as they got.

5

ELECTRIC POISON

The band's first European date was appropriately bizarre: an Ethiopian famine benefit at the Stowhill Labour Club, a working men's club in the small Welsh town of Newport, on October 3 1985. A flyer advises that only soft drinks will be served in the dancehall, while the members' bar elsewhere on the premises is "strictly members only". That almost certainly excluded any Buttholes-loving Welsh punks or curious members of the music press up from London.

Reviewing for the NME, Jack Barron wrote that "Singer Gibby, long hair trapped by a hundred clothes pegs, surrealism in shit row, mounts a chair, grabs his tongue and theatrical blood spurts; strips to underpants, fondles genitals, gore seeps from his crotch; puts on torn grandma's dress, fixes audience with blank stare and spews electric poison from a megaphone." Insisting that Leary's guitar "tears polka-dot hallucinations from the air," he describes the band's overall impact as "acidic core-hard overdrive that makes your ears flap in ecstasy... Beefheart, the Virgin Prunes, Residents, Dead Kennedys, Hawkwind and the Mothers of Invention all naked and rolling around in a bestial orgy."

To coincide with the European tour, the band also released a new EP via UK label Fundamental. While not officially released in the US until January 1986, Touch And Go issued a domestic "pre-release edition" in a plain green sleeve to counter leaks and piracy. Titled *Cream Corn From The Socket Of Davis*, the record's cover was originally intended to show just that; cream corn spewing from the socket of legendary one-eyed Rat Pack hoofer Sammy Davis Jr. But apparently when this image was recreated the results didn't meet the band's expectations, so instead, for the official US release, they used a blown-up photo of a girl child in a purple chiffon party dress; all the more disturbing for its suburban normality, contrasting with the music within. The UK release featured a head shot of a stern, matronly woman in horn-rimmed glasses, conceivably the little girl's mother.

The EP opens with the Buttholes' first big college radio airplay hit. 'Moving to Florida' is close cousin, probably incestuous, to 'Lady Sniff', a deformed, denatured blues parody seemingly narrated by a drooling, senile old man. Randomly intercut with sections of rapid-fire rock'n'roll, it is endlessly quotable once you can understand what Gibby's saying, spieling inspired non-sequiturs like "I'm going to have to potty train Chairman Mao", "Sausages dance like Ray Bolger on the hood of a car in a traffic jam", and so on.*

'Comb' – titled 'Lou Reed' on the UK release – is a dragging industrial noise piece with manipulated, distorted, unintelligible vocals. 'To Parter', AKA 'Two Part' is a prime example of the band's trademark unhinged, nightmarish folk-rock, with Gibby hollering about how all the sailors are junkies and the white man giving Quaaludes to the monkeys, as a two-guitar jam grows ever stormier and more intense behind him. A candidate for any Butthole Surfers 'Best Of' collection, the song would remain a staple of the band's live sets pretty much throughout their career. Finally, 'Tornadoes' is a frenzied two and a half minutes of screamin' and hollerin' and fretboard abuse.

Recorded in New York in September 1984, with Terence Smart on bass and both King and Teresa on drums, 'To Parter' and 'Tornadoes' were originally intended to be part of the band's next album for Alternative Tentacles, the provisionally titled *Rembrandt Pussy Horse*. But with Alternative Tentacles still unable or unwilling to release the album, and new product needed to promote in Europe, the

---

* Ray Bolger: Hollywood song-and-dance man best known for playing the Scarecrow in The Wizard Of Oz. Could there be a link here to Sammy Davis Jr, or indeed the song 'Tornadoes'?

Surfers hastily recorded the extra two tracks at their home studio in Winterville to make up an EP.

By the end of 1985, the Butthole Surfers lifestyle once again took its toll as, after a few US dates following their return from Europe, both Kramer – suffering from food poisoning – and Teresa Nervosa – stressed out, and later to suffer from strobe-induced seizures and a brain aneurysm – left the band. They were replaced in the new year by bassist Jeff Pinkus, formerly of Atlanta band Drowning In The Fountain, and another female drummer, Kytha Gernatt, generally known simply as Kabbage.

Kabbage had been a member of Atlanta's radical queer experimental music collective Easturn Stars, alongside the Buttholes' Atlanta friend Kathleen Lynch. The group was formed around local legend Benjamin Smoke, but there was no fixed line-up in terms of who played what. Jeff Pinkus insists that the Buttholes recruited Kabbage by accident, actually meaning to get Kathleen to join them on drums, but wires got crossed and, as they were crashing in Kabbage's Atlanta loft at the time, it seemed the easiest course to bring her on board. As it turned out, Kabbage wasn't a particularly good drummer, but her tenure did at least mean that Kathleen – by now working as 'Ta Da the Shit Lady' in a Times Square sex club – came back into contact with the group.

Kathleen's first onstage appearance with the band was at the most notorious and infamous of Butthole Surfers shows, at New York's Danceteria on February 7 1986. Much of what went on that night has already passed into legend, with all of the exaggeration and Chinese-whispers style distortion of the truth that suggests. The facts, as much as can be ascertained, are these: the band had been promised six thousand dollars for two shows on consecutive nights, and had driven cross country from California only to be told on arrival that the second show had been cancelled – along with, presumably, half their paycheck. Pissed off, they all proceeded to get even more wasted than usual before the performance.

Gibby: "Ten minutes into the show, I'd put on ten dresses – you see, I used to put dresses on and then tear 'em all off. But I'd gotten so tripping and so drunk I forgot to put on my underwear. So I got down to my last dress and, goddamn it, I was naked." By this time Kathleen had climbed onstage from the audience and had begun dancing around and removing her clothes until she too was completely naked. And bald. "And all of a sudden it became this sexual thing," Gibby continued. "There I was, with a semi-erect penis onstage, in between this girl's legs, and about to do this thing. Then it kinda suddenly dawned on me what was going on and I was like, woah!"

According to Paul Leary, who had previously been occupied in slashing all the speakers with a screwdriver, Gibby "mounted" a prone Kathleen while he was playing a lengthy guitar solo, her legs and Gibby's bare ass rising and falling through the strobes and the smoke, which came both from the dry ice machine and a small bonfire that had been lit on stage. "It's really fuckin' hideous," he recalled. One fan claimed he heard that Gibby thumb-fucked Kathleen's ass for forty-five minutes. Certainly, at one point Gibby fell into King's drums, knocking them over, and later Paul and Gibby were both drumming, after King had seemingly wandered off.

The show also saw the debut of the Butthole Surfer's infamous 'piss wands'. A toy plastic baseball bat, on this occasion with a Fred Flintstone theme, was urinated into by either Kabbage or Gibby, or both, and Kabbage started swinging it around while Gibby was occupied with Kathleen, 'anointing' the audience with their special water. When the band came offstage there was more trouble, with Gibby apparently repeatedly signing cheques for their $3000 dollar fee and then tearing them up. Further altercations resulted in Gibby being thrown naked out through the back door onto the wintry New York streets in the early hours of the morning. Supposedly the promoter told them they'd never play in the city again. They were booked into CBGBs the following week, and claim to have been paid more money, too.

Meanwhile, Alternative Tentacles were still refusing to release – or to even acknowledge – the album that the Butthole Surfers had submitted to them. *Rembrandt Pussy Horse* had largely been recorded at BOSS in San Antonio before the band hit the trail, as a continuation of the sessions for their debut. Despite the band's seeming defection to Touch And Go, Alternative Tentacles still held an option on this material, but for whatever reason they didn't seem in a hurry to put it out.

SCATOLOGICAL ALCHEMY

"*Rembrandt Pussy Horse* does not exist, has never existed and will never exist," they told the media as rumours began to spread. Faced with this impasse, the band cut their losses with Alternative Tentacles for good, remixed the existing recordings, and added a couple more tracks to replace the two that had been released on *Cream Corn From The Socket Of Davis*. *Rembrandt Pussyhorse* – note the subtle name change – finally came out on Touch And Go in April 1986.

The album was a huge step forward for the band, finally elevating them out of the hardcore ghetto and transcending their influences. With *Rembrandt Pussyhorse*, the Butthole Surfers finally nailed their own sound: a dark, compelling mixture of psychedelia, avant-garde noise rock and a sick, surreal sense of humour. Some found the album disappointingly mild, compared to the Buttholes' previous releases and their increasingly outrageous live shows, and certainly there were no full-on bouts of abrasive noise or frenzied punk thrashes. But few could argue that the LP wasn't the band's most consistent release. One gothic, unsettling mood dominates, in contrast to the almost schizophrenic switching between styles on previous records. That approach now seemed like a sequence of deliberate parodies, sketches or exercises in the band finding a style of its own. That quest found its culmination in this album, their first truly original, compelling creation.

Not that *Rembrandt Pussyhorse* is without its nods to records of the past. But this backwoods post-modernism has become an intrinsic element of the band's work, in the way that sampling is an integral part of hip-hop: a comment on or re-positioning of the original, rather than a mere rip-off. So the opening track 'Creep In The Cellar' itself opens with a sepulchral rendering of the familiar piano chords to Neil Young's 'Heart Of Gold'.

In 1986 there was nothing cool about referencing Neil Young, especially not his 1972 number one single that, in its FM radio ubiquity, seemed to represent everything that punk was set up to destroy. An archetypal slice of early seventies, Laurel Canyon singer-songwriter acoustic introspection, the song had more in common with Me Generation MOR minstrels James Taylor and Linda Ronstadt (both of whom sang backing vocals on the single), than the ragged, raging rockers Young would produce with Crazy Horse, his best-loved backing band.

Yet Young reacted against the popularity of 'Heart of Gold' by deliberately retreating from the middle of the road to "the ditch", as he put it, creating a sequence of dark, troubled, uncompromising and uncommercial mid-seventies albums that are now viewed as his finest work. It's these records that *Rembrandt Pussyhorse* shares some indirect common ground with, in that the album sees the Butthole Surfers' dark, modal folk tendencies in their fullest early flower. The 'Heart Of Gold' chord sequence represents a certain gloomy introspection, and the stark piano and cellar setting also recall Young's 'After The Goldrush', with its scene-setting opening line, "I was lying in a burned-out basement..."

It's not a heart of gold Gibby is searching for, though, but the demon within. "There's a creep in the cellar that I'm gonna let in," he declares, and so we see him descending the stairs into the sub-basement of his unconsciousness, to unlock whatever repressed, evil, monstrous persona is lurking down there. "He really freaks me out when he peels off his skin," Gibby admits, not to mention how he starts talking backwards with his head spinning around. Nevertheless, this is the Buttholes' prime mission: to free the inner creep, no matter how sick, horrific or distasteful he or she might seem to be.

The song also prominently features backwards violin playing; to save money, the group had recorded over existing tape at BOSS, and the fiddles, from an old session by an unknown country and western group, came through on an unused track. They worked so well that they kept them, running them backwards for further freaky effect. Incidentally, the piano is played by Bob O'Neill himself, who plays all the keyboard parts on the album.

'Sea Ferring', the next song, is one of the two numbers recorded later and added to the album after the *Cream Corn From The Socket Of Davis* EP was released. This and 'Mark Says Alright' are the only Butthole Surfers studio tracks to feature Trevor Malcolm on bass (Leary plays bass on the rest of the album, with the exception of 'American Woman', which features Terence Smart). This haunted shanty is an early example of the wobbly, unstable sound that would become a Butthole Surfers trademark: pounding, bowing and bending, like an unworthy vessel on stormy waters, the song contemplates the chaos that underlies the seemingly ordered surface of existence. "Is life as strange as it seems? It lies on its side as it dreams... The earth screams like a madman." Later, Gibby launches into a series of absurd similes that seem to be laid out like some stream of consciousness word association game: "Like a seahorse, like a grey dawn, like a moron... like a housewife, like a rapist, like a tea cup, like a dustpan..."

Having referenced one Canadian rock classic on 'Creep In The Cellar', the Buttholes take on another in their astonishing deconstruction of the Guess Who's 'American Woman'.* Irreverent doesn't begin to describe it; the track is mostly stripped back to severely gated, possibly reversed drums that are absurdly high in the mix, echoing the avant-garde drum sound of the early PiL albums that had become, thanks to Phil Collins, the default sound of mid-eighties Adult-Oriented Rock.† Yet the Buttholes' version returns to the strangeness of early dub, and the beats almost sound cut-and-pasted, hip-hop style.

Where the Guess Who's chubby frontman Burton Cummings sang in a blues Viking style midway between Robert Plant and Jim Morrison, Gibby sing-speaks in a high-pitched squeak that completely undermines the macho protest of the original. Leary's squealing guitar mangles the familiar riff, and midway through Gibby begins barking through a megaphone as though mishandling a delicate hostage situation. "No man is an island, so come on out of there," he commands, and suddenly he's like some naked, shit-smeared RD Laing, using shock tactics to break down all the personal barriers and individual inhibitions that keep us separate and isolated. The Guess Who were protesting about

---

* It's tempting to read the band's decision to pick on Canadian rock culture in particular as reflecting the origins of bassist Trevor Malcolm; unfortunately, both 'Creep In The Cellar' and 'American Woman' predate his membership in the band.
† Collins' trademark "gated reverb" drum sound, as premiered on his multi-million selling 1981 single 'In The Air Tonight', was directly influenced by Public Image Limited. But their *Flowers of Romance* album – also 1981 – featured a drum sound that was in turn partly inspired by the effects used by producer Hugh Padgham for Collins' drumming on the track 'Intruder', from Peter Gabriel's third self-titled album (1980). The Butthole Surfers are known fans of Public Image Limited; their opinions on Phil Collins are unknown.

the cultural dominance of their giant super-powered neighbour, but for the Butthole Surfers it's not about American or Canadian identity, but transcending all the labels, prejudices and politics that conspire to keep us apart.

The album continues with the driving, one-chord piano line of 'Waiting For Jimmy To Kick', over which sinister, muffled voices occasionally break into cackling laughter. The effect is like listening in to a private phone conversation that suddenly turns dark and psychotic; the sort of situation that would appeal to the filmmaker David Lynch. 'Strangers Die Every Day' is high gothic, with more muffled, distorted vocals repeating the title over a descending arpeggio played on a reverberating church organ. These voices are then submerged in babbling static, and the sound of gently lapping water somehow sounds impossibly dank and fetid.

Loosely based on the theme music to the popular TV detective show *Perry Mason*, 'Perry' is churning, carnival freakshow rock over which Gibby gives Perry the news in a bad English accent, seemingly via the telephone. "It's talking about being the slave boy – it's talking about giving head when you're six years old," he recites. Then, "Cancer! Cancer! Cancer!" gleefully and hysterically, before breaking down into manic laughter and honking clown horns.

It's as though Gibby is telling Perry what life is really all about; the great sick joke at the heart of the Butthole Surfers' work, the black cosmic giggle of a depraved and amoral God, toying with humanity like a schoolboy casually burning the wings off of flies. "It's about coming of age, it's about growing up... it's about licking the shit off the walls, it's about doing the things you're supposed to do. It's about being a Butthole Surfer. It's about promotional work..." The Butthole Surfers are vicious psychedelic satirists, Gibby Haynes a punk rock Lenny Bruce, saying the unsayable in the name of tearing the veil from our eyes, laying it bare like Billy Burroughs, the Naked Lunch; the moment we all really see what's quivering on the end of our fork. As the music concludes in a squeal of feedback, the vocals continue, ending the song on a note of plaintive, acid-damaged pathos: "The little bits of crayon, the melted pieces, the loving friends; all the things you wish you had."

The queasy drone of 'Whirling Hall Of Knives' echoes the medieval acid trip side of *The Velvet Underground And Nico*, 'Black Angel's Death Song' in particular. Borrowing its title from a track off Grand Funk Railroad's 1970 *Live Album*, 'Mark Says Alright' features pit bull Mark Farner on lead vocals, growling over a sinister, noir-ish, tripwire-tense funk jam that recalls the English goth band Bauhaus. The album ends with a "dub" reprise of 'Creep In The Cellar', titled simply 'In The Cellar'. The creep is no longer confined there; he is free and roaming among you now and it's too late to re-capture and restrain him. There's no going back.

There is a theory that *Rembrandt Pussyhorse* actually features subliminal sounds that have a psychological or even physical effect upon the listener that they can't consciously account for. According to this unverified urban myth, the album deliberately employs a certain bass frequency that puts the listener into a bad mood, making them feel depressed, annoyed, angry or even nauseous. There's no real evidence for this, apart from the many people who have felt their mood change abruptly for the worse upon listening to the album. Personally, although I feel it's a great record, it's not one that I play often as it does tend to have this effect on me. Of course, once one knows about the subliminal frequencies theory, the effect could be self-perpetuating. Nevertheless, *Rembrandt Pussyhorse* is an extremely dark and twisted album that probably shouldn't be listened to while driving or operating heavy machinery. As for experiencing it on mind-altering chemicals, this is probably only advisable if you're the kind of masochist who enjoys that kind of fucked-up fun. As the saying almost goes: in your own head be it.

6
SATAN! SATAN! SATAN!

The very day that *Rembrandt Pussyhorse* was released, on April 18 1986, the Butthole Surfers underwent yet another line-up change. Driving up to New York for a show at Irving Plaza the next night, they had dumped the hapless Kabbage, dropping her off near her parents' home in Knoxville, Tennessee as they passed through. The band went on to tour Europe as a four-piece, a period that also saw Touch And Go release the live video *Blind Eye Sees All*.

Comprising of footage culled from two shows the band played in Detroit on February 22 and March 3 1985, the film was already out-of-date as a representation of the band's live show and line-up. Shot on flat eighties videotape, with no regard for continuity in the editing (note those rapid-fire costume changes!), the set predates the Buttholes' use of lights, smoke and projections, and the theatrics are decidedly improvised and low budget. Nevertheless, the performances are impressively raw, particularly King and Teresa's leaping, flailing, drumming tag team. The tape is also the only official documentation of Trevor Malcolm's time in the band. He comes over as a dapper blonde beatnik boy and Andy Warhol lookalike, surprisingly at home during the hilarious bed-in interview sequences. These are notable for Gibby's bizarre collapsing haystack hair and his gift for free-flowing, surrealist, verbal improvisation – obvious in his songs of course, but just as impressive in the raw.

On April 26, the Buttholes played Klub Foot at the Clarendon Ballroom in London, but a screw-up over work permits meant that a second London show, at Dingwalls two nights later, was cancelled. The band managed seven shows in mainland Europe – the Netherlands, Belgium, Germany and Denmark – that were notable for Paul's psychedelically-patterned bellbottom trousers and a spirited rendition of Gordon Lightfoot's 'The Wreck Of The Edmund Fitzgerald'. Oh, and they were also arrested in Belgium for what were initially thought to be rape charges. In fact, they were in legal disagreement with the tour manager, when the band pulled out of several shows after learning that they weren't getting paid. Something was lost in translation, something was misinterpreted as 'rape' and the band were apparently escorted from the country by armed police, though never charged with any crime.

After the eventful European tour, the band finally decided that it was time to settle down, back home on the range in Texas. They found a two-bedroom house at 1401 East Anderson Lane in Austin, right next to Interstate Highway 183 where it crosses Cameron Road, which they nicknamed the Compound and fitted out as a rehearsal space, eight-track recording studio, and living quarters. With the entire band moving in, conditions were cramped, even when they added primitive 'lofts' –false ceilings made of plywood on which it was possible to bed down. "I lived in the master bedroom closet," recalled Jeff Pinkus. "Paul lived above the console, King had a mattress that he put on the wall that he slept on in the live room, and Gibby had a loft up above the hallway that connected the two rooms…"

It was at the Compound that the band recorded much of their next album, 1987's *Locust Abortion Technician*. Parts of the record had already been recorded in Georgia, but those tracks were remixed at the compound as new material was added. The band also managed to convince Teresa to re-join them, and she moved into the Compound, sharing a loft with Gibby and playing on the new album.

"We had a Sony Betamax and a PCM machine for our digital recorder," Jeff said. "Usually the poorest version of whatever somebody had, but we learned how to work with whatever we had." It was a step down from the sixteen-track facilities at BOSS, but the limitations, such as only having one microphone, forced the band to become more creative. Plus, home recording gave them more time and freedom to experiment – and to take large quantities of drugs.

Locust Abortion Technician, released in March 1987, is perhaps the band's finest album. It's certainly their heaviest and most extreme, though on first listen it may seem to lack the depth, complexity and songwriting of *Rembrandt Pussyhorse*. But this is only because the Buttholes have now, for the most part, gone beyond songs, into uncharted sonic territory that bears only a slight resemblance to whatever we may have previously considered music. This isn't punk, goth, industrial or heavy metal, though it certainly incorporates elements of all of those genres. This is the Butthole Surfers in full-on acid psychosis mode; like nothing much that had come before, and where mercifully few have dared to follow since.

It opens with deceptive gentleness. The introduction to 'Sweat Loaf' glides and glistens into being, and the experience for the listener is like peacefully awakening from a pleasant dream. A child asks a question: "Daddy? What does regret mean?" The father answers, in a paternal, avuncular and just slightly creepy voice that the funny thing about regret is that it's better to regret something you have done than to regret something that you haven't done. And then comes the rude awakening: "And by the way, if you see your mom this weekend, will you be sure to tell her – SATAN! SATAN! SATAN!"

Employing an old Black Sabbath riff much as one might use a rusty kitchen knife as a makeshift scalpel, the Butthole Surfers prise open your mucus-encrusted third eye. Look! See the horror! Gentle finger-picking interludes offer only a teasing illusion of respite. The song is another of the band's deconstructions of neglected rock classics, following their assault upon the Guess Who's 'American Woman' on *Rembrandt Pussyhorse*. The source here is 'Sweet Leaf', Black Sabbath's ode to the joys of pot smoking from their third LP, 1971's *Master Of Reality*.

Like Neil Young, Black Sabbath would enjoy critical rehabilitation in the nineties, when they were revered as a prototype for grunge, but they were far from cool in 1987. The Surfers' use of them as a reference point is deliberately perverse; Black Sabbath, by the late eighties, represented rock in all its unfashionable, unreconstructed grossness. This was party music for small-town hicks, here shoved right back in the face of all of the post-punk hipsters who thought themselves far too cool and cultured to enjoy such dumb thrills. But the Butthole Surfers recognised in Black Sabbath the very primal ooze of rock, and knew that stupidity was as much its essence as energy or darkness.

The song's impact is monstrous. The churning guitar riff is distorted and brutal, and Gibby's vocals are rendered near-unintelligible by his 'Gibbytronix' – a recently acquired electronic effects unit that enabled him to speed up, slow down and otherwise alter his voice, debuted to frightening, disorienting effect on the band's spring '86 tour. The result is a nightmarish reinvention of rock, actually transforming it into the terrifying satanic force right-wing Christian fundamentalists appeared to hear when they railed against toothless, airbrushed pap of the day like Motley Crue, Twisted Sister or, indeed, former Black Sabbath frontman Ozzy Osbourne's solo albums.

Next up is the crushingly slowed-down 'Graveyard', with the vocals in particular reduced to a dragged-out groan over pounding drums and warped guitar gnarl. The track is revisited on side two of the album, but at this early stage of this record it's simply a disorienting bombardment. We're all lying in the graveyard, rotting away, and we can't understand what Gibby or the band are saying, because we aren't tuned in to their frequency yet. On the original vinyl album, it's unclear as to whether this song should actually be played at 45RPM; doing so certainly makes it sound more intelligible and "normal". But then you find that most of the songs on the album make at least as much sense at the wrong speed anyway.

'Pittsburgh To Lebanon', AKA 'Shotgun', pushes macho blues clichés to the limit, being a churning, overdriven take on the likes of Muddy Waters' 'Manish Boy' or Bo Diddley's 'Who Do You Love'. "I bought my first shotgun at the age of thirteen," Gibby snarls menacingly, before suggesting that the road of excess might lead to the palace of wisdom after all: "Wine whisky and women, Lord, by the time that I was five/I said, Lord, the way that I'm living, you know I might wind up alive."

The eerie high-pitched backing vocals, by the way, echo Peter Green's Fleetwood Mac on their devil-haunted classic, 'Green Manalishi' – one of the last tracks the troubled singer-guitarist cut with the band before descending into the acid-induced, career-crippling clutches of serious mental illness.

'Hay' is all surface noise: human cattle, small talk, meaningless greetings, social static. Yet coded within it, in the rapid backwards scratching and sinister bass glide, is the DNA of the album's still-to-be-revealed final track. 'Hay' and '22 Going On 23' are basically the same recording, cut up and arranged in different ways and at different pitch and speed. 'Hay' appears innocuous, its title suggesting both the passivity of grazing farm animals and the "Hey" with which human beings acknowledge each other without really thinking or engaging. Yet, by the album's end, the full horror beneath the mindless surface will have been revealed, a horror that subliminally existed within this track all along.

The only real song on side one is the closer, but what a song it is. 'Human Cannonball' is a neglected classic of late eighties alternative rock, and it's a great shame that its planned single release was abandoned, as it matches and even trumps indie hits of the era by bands like the Jesus And Mary Chain or Dinosaur Jr. Starting out with a strangled cry of "Are you ready to rock?" and a driving mod-punk-surf beat, it initially recalls the Ramones, or bubblegum pop like the Shadows Of Knight's 'Shake', or even cheesy glam rock by the Sweet ('Ballroom Blitz') or Suzi Quatro ('Devilgate Drive').

Yes it's pop, but twisted, tormented, dirtied up by Paul Leary's Crazy Horse guitar riffs and Gibby's hoarse, demented finger-in-ear folkie holler. "Pardon me, I'm only bleeding," he caterwauls, "but you cut me to the bone." It's as close as the Butthole Surfers get to a love song. "Now you must be feeling like a human cannonball." Catchy as hell, the song was going to be released as a seven-inch with a B-side featuring the Butthole Surfers "Greatest Hits" – every song they'd ever recorded (all 32 of them) all playing simultaneously. Tragically, this dream was never realised.

Side two opens with 'USSA', the sound of running, marching feet, revving engines and heroically warped guitar, over which Gibby repeatedly chants the song's title in a distressed scream. If this is political it's all implied, but what's implied isn't pretty. Certainly Gibby sounds like he's being placed under extreme duress – torture, brainwashing. And does the title conflate the USA with its Cold War nemesis, the Union of Soviet Socialist Republics – dubbed "the Evil Empire" by President Reagan in a 1983 speech – or the notorious 'SS' of Nazi Germany?*

'The O-Men' is utterly demented, pure Texas psychedelia, lost in a bad trip on too much peyote and trucker speed, with Gibby speaking in tongues like a possessed redneck in the grip of furious demons while the band rage unheeding behind him. They follow this with 'Kuntz', an entire song lifted from an obscure compilation of Thai folk-pop, but molested and tampered with, all with the objective of highlighting what sounds like a very rude word in the original song's chorus.

The word that sounds like "cunt" is in fact "khan" in the original song, and translates as an itch that the singer desperately wants to scratch. Written by Kong Katkamhaeng and performed by Phloen Phromdaen, the song is completely uncredited on the album, and essentially functions as a hip-hop style sample, but a sample that forms a whole song. In 1987 the use of samples was still controversial and legally dubious, and it was not uncommon for them to be uncredited on a record. The Butthole Surfers' use of the track recalls not only the post-modern art music of the Residents from a decade earlier, but also contemporary artists like Steinski and Mass Media (on 'The Motorcade Sped On'), the Justified Ancients of Mu Mu (later to become the KLF) and Negativland, who used sampling and cut-up collaging to make a political point or for the sake of social commentary, rather than for musical reasons. Admittedly however, the Buttholes only point here is to make a dirty schoolboy joke – unless one chooses to make a case

---

* It's worth recalling that this was the era during which the US Government illegally supported the Contras in their rebellion against the Nicaraguan Government, and that US advisors were found to have actively encouraged human rights violations such as kidnapping and torture. The Iran-Contra scandal came to light during 1986, while *Locust Abortion Technician* was being recorded. Additionally, at the beginning of his second term of office in 1985, Reagan visited Germany and laid a wreath at the Bitburg Cemetery, which contained the graves of 49 Waffen SS soldiers – an incident that inspired a rare political song from the ordinarily goofy Ramones, 'Bonzo Goes To Bitburg'.

that they're satirically commenting on the cultural appropriation of ethnic music by western artists and self-appointed experts, which I think might be over-crediting the band.

A second reading of 'Graveyard' finds Leary's guitar grinding over Jeff Pinkus' catchy stoner-goth bassline, in what is now a relatively accessible piece of rusty sludge rock – or have we just become accustomed to their wavelength? Before we have time to wonder about this however the album closes with its most notorious track.

'22 Going On 23', opens with a recording taken from a radio phone-in show, in which a woman talks about being unable to sleep since she was sexually assaulted. Billowing guitar noise rises up behind her like the gates of Hell have opened, spewing out over a heavy, oppressive beat. "Depression-anxiety-counselling-medicine" a voice repeats, echoing uselessly in the void. And then Leary penetrates the murk with an astonishing modal guitar solo that is positively hymnal; mourning our pain but also seeming to offer some kind of absolution.

'22 Going On 23' is an uncomfortable listen. At first one might think that the phone-in sample is being used as part of a bad frat-boy joke, that the band are inviting us to laugh at this woman talking about being sexually assaulted, in yet another example of their famously sick, amoral sense of humour. But in fact, nothing about '22 Going On 23' sounds like a joke. Taken in its own right – that is, away from any context one might associate with a band calling itself the Butthole Surfers – it sounds like a powerful and accurate expression of rage, horror and pity at the society we've created, a society where experiences like the one being described are almost the norm rather than the exception, and are made all the more traumatic for being routinely swept under the carpet.

It's also important to note here that the band claimed that the phone-in was a fake; that is, it was recorded from a genuine radio show, but the woman was a regular caller who invented a different problem every time she called. This may excuse the band from charges of being exploitative, or not; even if their account is true, this is still a recording of a mentally disturbed woman being used without her knowledge or consent, though not exactly for the purposes of entertainment. This is artistic catharsis, and ultimately – in my opinion – the end result is good and powerful enough to justify the means.

"When I have these bad dreams I try to put endings on the dream where I come out a winner," the caller continues hesitantly. "But I can't seem to do that. I keep having the same dream over and over." In the Butthole Surfers' worldview, human existence is one long recurring nightmare in which we endlessly and hopelessly struggle to come out on top, instead of actually trying to awaken, which is what they've been violently encouraging us to do all along.

Another woman talks about how she watches a soap opera every day, then turns it off in shame and embarrassment when her husband walks through the door. She longs to travel, but her husband says he did all the travelling he needed while in the service. A Greek chorus of mooing cattle give rather heavy-handed notice that this typical couple are sleepwalking through their benighted experience, representing everything sedentary and repressed that the Butthole Surfers stand in opposition to.

This theme of awakening – from comforting dream into reality's nightmare, and then finally from out of the nightmare to some greater cosmic truth – runs throughout *Locust Abortion Technician*, and indeed through all of the band's work. From the soporific opening and sudden rude awakening of 'Sweat Loaf', to the death-in-life imagery of 'Graveyard' and 'Pittsburgh to Lebanon', to the pained grace of Paul's final guitar solo.

Paul's performance here taps into the same soulful energy source as Hendrix's 'Star-Spangled Banner' or Eddie Hazel's playing on Funkadelic's mighty 'Maggot Brain'. Though relatively simple, it recalls the contorted, expressive playing of the great proponents of free jazz, Albert Ayler or Ornette Coleman. Rising heavenward from out of the fuzz of feedback and abject existential misery, it transforms the whole album from a squalid experience to an uplifting one; a trial by fire and iron certainly, but one from which one emerges stronger and wiser.

The band would claim that *Locust Abortion Technician* was just a random juxtaposition of words, chosen for jarring and unsettling effect, just as *Rembrandt Pussyhorse* was. This may be the case, but could it also be relevant that the locust is a Biblical symbol of the end times? Could a locust abortion technician then be trying to avert the apocalypse as described in the Book of Revelation, when "From the smoke came locusts on the earth... on their heads were what looked like crowns of gold; their faces were like human faces, their hair like women's hair, and their teeth like lions' teeth."

Also worth noting is the album's cover art; 'Fido and the Clowns', a 1980 painting by Arthur Sarnoff – not, as rumoured, clown-obsessed serial killer John Wayne Gacy. Sarnoff was a prolific advertising artist in the 1950s, and was also famous for his kitsch paintings of dogs playing pool. But even without the Gacy connection, the contrasts between this overly-innocent painting, the album title and the sounds within are creepy enough. Also, many people are terrified of clowns; though ostensibly jolly figures of fun meant to entertain children, they also tap into something distinctly dark, buried in the subconscious. Come to think of it, that description could fit the Butthole Surfers as well.

The album brought the band to a new level of public awareness, particularly in Britain, where it was their first to be distributed by Paul Smith's Blast First label. Their Blast First labelmates included Sonic Youth and Big Black, and, along with kindred spirits like Swans and Live Skull, these bands were often grouped together as part of a wave of abrasive American noise bands – post-hardcore, pre-grunge, and more experimental than both. Frequent radio-play by revered British DJ John Peel helped, and many first heard '22 Going On 23' when it was voted to number 44 in his Festive Fifty for 1987.

The Butthole Surfers were gradually getting noticed outside of the DIY post-punk scene. Late in 1986, after completing *Locust Abortion Technician,* the band found themselves in the studio with comedienne Sandra Bernhard, attempting a version of Heart's 'Barracuda'. Sadly, this would never see the light of day. "Sandra had a crush on Teresa, like everybody did," Jeff Pinkus explained. "We met her at her show in Austin, and Teresa went back and talked to her, so we ended up hanging out all night with her at some weird gay bar." Bernhard even told the entire primetime nation, when she was a guest on *Late Night With David Letterman*, that she'd been "hanging out with the Butthole Surfers." According to Pinkus, her vocals were so awful that the track was unusable, though an alternate recording did eventually surface with Bernhard singing perfectly well, albeit in Spanish. If anything, the track is a bit too polished and commercial for 1986 vintage Buttholes, with a streamlined sheen and a steady drum machine rhythm, over which Bernhardt wails quasi-operatically. An English language version might have given the Butthole Surfers a crossover hit; in reality, however, the band were destined to spend a few more years on the fringes of cultural acceptability before any kind of crossover would happen.

7
CRAZY GODDAMN WORLD

Though Kathleen had occasionally danced onstage with the Buttholes since her notorious debut at the Danceteria, she joined them full-time for the spring 1987 tour promoting *Locust Abortion Technician* across the US. Far more than just another naked go-go dancer, Lynch was more frightening than sexy. Bald and shaved all over, her moves bore as much relation to traditional burlesque routines as the Butthole Surfers' music did to the toe-tapping tunes of the Top 40. Her specialities included bizarre wigs (on both her head and pubis), freakish body paint and Dadaist props such as tennis rackets on her feet. Kathleen's performances ramped up the overall weirdness, and certainly weren't intended to titillate; in the photo used on the cover of the Buttholes' *Double Live* album, for instance, she made an all-too convincing space alien.

Kathleen had a unique philosophy when it came to body hygiene; basically, she was against it. Even the Butthole Surfers found it an endurance test to be stuck in a cramped van with her on a 20-hour drive between shows. She rarely washed herself or her clothes, and loved shit, urine and all the things of the body. She loved B.O. and dirty underwear; the band had to hold her down to do her laundry, while she screamed and struggled in protest. When she and the rest of the band got scabies, she adopted the parasites as pests and refused to be medicated.

Kathleen earned the nickname of 'Ta-Dah The Shit Lady' while working in a Times Square peepshow. One evening, suffering from food poisoning while nude and performing, she accidentally fired a projectile shit against the wall. All she could think to do was make it part of the act by immediately standing tall and proclaiming "Ta-Dah!" The customer ran from the booth screaming, but the 80-year-old proprietor knew a gimmick when she saw one and added it to her pitch outside the club: "Step right up folks; we got white chicks, we got black chicks, we got Mexican chicks, and we even got the Shit Lady!"

In August, Kathleen joined the Butthole Surfers on a European tour for the first time. The band returned to Newport, where the support bands included badly miscast indie poppers the Darling Buds, as well as West Country cidercore trio Dadi Janki. Their then-teenage drummer Jennie Howell remembers the Buttholes' set as "A compelling, intense, immersive, mind/spirit-altering happening." The jaunt also included a notorious London date, once more at the Clarendon Ballroom, on the hottest night of the summer. With many fans left queuing on the pavements outside, sweat ran down the walls and dry ice choked the packed upstairs room, and when Gibby began setting fire to cymbals people started desperately trying to get away from the stage. Paul Leary described the gig as one of the worst the band ever played, and while technical problems led to a somewhat truncated set, many who were there still regard it as a landmark, life-changing event. It's clear that the Butthole Surfers were now at their peak as a live band, so that even on an off-night they could be terrifyingly spectacular.

"I'd been to Big Black's last ever British gig at the same venue a month before, when the fire limit was seriously compromised, and it was a similar tale for the Buttholes, only they were actually setting things on fire," remembers Jim Fedrick, a member of the audience that night. "They started by flooding the entire venue with dry ice, to the extent that you could barely make out the person stood next to you. They then turned all regular lighting off, and replaced it with a strobe. It was like being inside a TV 'snowstorm'. I remember being at the front, surrounded by Dutch people, banging off their collective nuts, speaking Dutch, which made it feel all the more alienating. Gibby started with his Jim Morrison 'walked on down the hall' pisstake, before arriving at 'Satan! Satan! Satan!' and straight into 'Sweat Loaf'. There followed an hour or so of cymbals aflame, Kathleen Lynch dancing naked and Austin Police Department videos of dead people being cut out of car wrecks, before they finished up with a properly deranged '22 Going On 23'. Amazing. Nearly thirty years ago, and I remember it like it was yesterday."

A show at Knopf's Music Hall in Hamburg was apparently even more oversold, and German punks who couldn't get in set fire to tyres and ended up battling with police. The date was supposed to be the start of a German mini-tour titled "Kings of Independence," and featuring a mouth-watering line-up headlined by Nick Cave and the Bad Seeds and also featuring Swans and the Fall. However, the Butthole Surfers pulled out of the remaining dates after the first one was so badly organised, and following personality clashes with some of the other musicians on the bill.

Kathleen wasn't with the band when they briefly came back to England at the beginning of 1988 for two London shows, one of which – at Harlesden Mean Fiddler – was filmed for a feature on the BBC's short-lived teatime alternative music show *Snub TV* (though the episode didn't run till the following year). Again, hundreds of fans who couldn't get in were escorted away by police, gaining the band further coverage in the weekly music press and the daily tabloids, the latter latching onto the band's sensationalist name and antics rather than their music. Nevertheless, all this served to help promote the Butthole Surfers' fourth album, *Hairway To Steven*, which was released in April of that year.

Hairway To Steven was recorded during December 1987 and January 1988 at January Sound studios in Dallas with the band's soundman, Ric Wallace, as co-producer. The songs, for the most part, were already written before the sessions began, and had all been introduced into the live set at various points during the previous year, with 'John E Smoke' dating back to the beginning of 1986 and Jeff Pinkus's introduction to the band. This meant that recording was quick and relatively painless, but it also meant that the album lacked some of the spontaneous, drug-crazed creativity of their previous work.

If a creeping professionalism and craft was starting to gnaw away at the Butthole Surfers, however, then the sleeve art did its best to be as weird and uncommercial as possible, by way of compensation. Apart from the obvious-but-brilliant title (a spoonerism of Led Zeppelin's perennial rock anthem 'Stairway to Heaven,' as if it needed explaining), there were no credits or song titles anywhere on the packaging, with songs denoted only by obscene illustrations on the original vinyl LP's centre label. The cover art was a grotesque gurning face, created by overlaying photographic headshots of all the band's members, one on top of the other. Song names were identified by fans from live set lists and later from 1989's *Double Live* album.

The record kicks off with what is perhaps its best shot, the oblique Hendrix tribute 'Jimi'. Over pounding drums and some of Paul Leary's most demented guitar playing, Gibby enacts a confrontation between an apparently abusive demon-father and his abused child, playing both parts via the pitch-shifting capabilities of his Gibbytronix. The demon persona almost seems to hark back to Anus Presley himself, from the band's first EP, while the imagery of Biblical apocalypse and sexual abuse link to themes on *Locust Abortion Technician*. The song also continues the Buttholes' exploration of the speed-changing possibilities of the vinyl record, sounding far more 'normal' and intelligible at 45RPM, but more pleasingly weird and freaky at 33 and a third.

"I'm soiled… soil me…" the song opens, before the demon lays out his rap: "I have come ten million miles and travelled on your earth; and with his hands the fiery beast may consummate my birth." There are references to plagues of flies and locusts before the terrified child-voice begins begging her father for help, pleading, "My mind is at an end."

"All hope is lost, you're bleeding now, your dreams forever flagged," the demon taunts, and then reveals his true identity: "What do you know about reality? I am reality!"

"Don't touch me on my penis and vagina," the suddenly hermaphroditic child pleads. "Don't touch me on my bottom, please daddy!" Then suddenly he/she's pained cries turn to manic laughter. "Crazy, crazy fucking world! What a crazy goddamned world we live in!"

"What's so funny?" the demon roars in retaliation, and the song builds to a nightmarish climax of squealing electronics and distorted guitars, pounding and squelching in a disturbing simulation of actual sonic buggery, before tolling church bells usher in the contrasting second part of the song; slightly clumsy but attractively melodic acoustic guitar-picking, mooing cows, barking dogs and crowing roosters, and still pitch-shifting, murmuring vocals. The mood now is pastoral and serene, not a million miles from mid-seventies Pink Floyd – if Pink Floyd had been brain-damaged, psychotic Texan road freaks, rather than middle-class Cambridge architecture students.

The song seems to be broadly about loss of innocence, though not necessarily sexual abuse. The 'abuser' is life itself, in the sense that as we get older, experience sees our childhood dreams trampled into the dust. This is a recurring theme in Butthole Surfers songs, but here the ultimate message is positive: if we can accept and even laugh at the nightmarish horrors of existence, then to a large extent they lose their power over us. The only salvation, the only saving grace, is just to laugh at what a crazy god-damned world it is. The sane alternative, after all, is suicide, which just proves that you've lost your sense of humour.

'Ricky' is a driving, seventies-styled hard rock song with a buried, wailing vocal that seems to be about an obsessive stalker and phone pest. It's enjoyable, but pretty throwaway. 'I Saw An X-Ray Of A Girl Passing Gas' is better, a folk-rock number that opens with three bars of droning vocals over bare drums, before the acoustic guitars kick in and the track lifts up towards a bathetic anthem of a chorus. The song seems to be set in a hospital and opens with Gibby getting an injection, which suggests that what follows is a mixed-up dream-vision experienced under anaesthetic. The stream of consciousness imagery is violent and apocalyptic, Gibby chanting "Hey, hey Daddy, why die in the war?" before rolling into "Jesus Hitler Buddha Santa Klaus Barbie Christ Moore" and "God Dog Sex Death Life" in what sounds like a parody of Sonic Youth's pseudo beat poetry on contemporary albums like *Bad Moon Rising* and *EVOL*. On the other hand, the song also abstractly conjures the familiar Buttholes theme of history as a nightmare from which we're trying to awake, with all our heaviest concepts being relative to each other and, ultimately, no more than that – just concepts.

Side two opens with the epic 'John E Smoke', its portentous bass and guitar glissando opening, over fake crowd roars, setting it up as a parody of a psychedelic stadium rock song – the sort of thing the Doors might have ended up doing if Jim Morrison had got out of the bath that day in 1971. Again, the lyrics seem like mock-profound stream of consciousness gibberish, recited over acoustic guitars and tribal drums, but if Gibby is just free associating, then it's hilarious, brilliant stuff, about how "John was a little crippled midget lesbian boy but he stood ten foot tall with a knife."

In this increasingly surreal fable, a mole appears on John's left leg, extending "over 469 different miles," and starts speaking to John "in 69 different languages" as it evolves into a legless dog. John protests to the dog that "I am not the magma, I am not the crust, and I shall evolve when the rain has come down here and washed on John." He claims that he'll be a cigarette butt – i.e., all burned out – before it's all done with, but the voices disagree and tell him "You are the flame itself and you shall burn pure in the South American sky where the blood dogs worship the self." Then the QE2 liner extends out of John's left side and John finally transcends his physical form – "His body was no longer the prime means to express himself" – and is pulled up to a higher state of existence by the dog's bleeding eyes, which "roped around John's leg and pulled him up, like he was a canoe."

Absurd as it is, the song sounds almost like an authentic aborigine legend, with symbolism so dense and coded, and probably mistranslated so many times by oral transmission down many generations of uneducated people, that it makes absolutely no sense to outsiders when they come across it. In this case the tribe is limited to the band themselves, and even they probably don't remember what it's meant to mean.

'Roky' was supposedly written for the mentally ill former 13th Floor Elevator singer Roky Erickson to sing, but he turned it down; if one listens to it with this in mind, then the track would seem to be about Roky too, as sung from the damaged singer's own point of view. "Well, all of my friends baby, they're going insane, now. Look up at my fingers, maybe get lost in the rain." The song is a classic, melodic folk-rock ballad, and the second verse seems to refer to Roky's own 'Click Your Fingers Applauding The Play', as well as his perceived mental health issues: "Well, all of my friends, baby, they say I'm insane, now; well, I'm snapping my fingers, darling, I'm cracking the reins."

An emotive bridge refers to "walking through the haze of scattered memories," which could indeed be an accurate observation of Roky's existence in Austin at that time, still suffering the after-effects of the electric shock treatment and anti-psychotic drugs he was given at the Rusk Maximum Security Unit for the Criminally Insane, after being arrested for possession of a single joint in 1969 and misguidedly pleading insanity. Similarly, "Afraid to hear the sound of all that's going down" could refer to his habit of drowning out the voices in his head with many different radios and TV sets all tuned to different stations, or alternatively to those around him who refuse to hear the disturbing messages in his songs.

Sadly, after this highpoint the album gradually peters out. 'Julio Iglesias' is a return to the band's occasional earlier rockabilly style, and is no more than a poor joke that should have stayed on the cutting room floor; 'Backass' is a great piece of grinding, pounding, anthemic industrial goth-psych, but it's somewhat one-dimensional and overstays its welcome. Finally, 'Fast' sounds like indigestion; bloated, slowed-down vocals and fizzing, sped up guitars. It's fine, but pretty disposable.

Hairway To Steven found the Butthole Surfers at a crucial juncture in their career. They were finally earning decent, regular money, were selling out shows wherever they went, and after three years of being essentially homeless, they were reasonably settled in Austin. In 1988 they moved from The Compound on 1401 Anderson to a five acre ranch in the Texas hill country of Driftwood, around thirty miles west of the city, where plentiful countryside and long, laid-back evenings of beer and barbecues worked their mellowing magic.

In short, the Butthole Surfers had survived their desperate punk years and were no longer living hand to mouth; they were professional musicians and had actually been able to make a career out of their drug-crazed, travelling freak show existence. As surprised as anyone by this, they now had to figure out how to sustain it, especially now that Gibby and Paul were hitting their 30s. They had about as much desire to go back to the squalor of no-budget touring as they did to get proper jobs. Leary in particular became a notorious workaholic, always driven to produce more, work harder, to keep the momentum going. So, to accuse the Buttholes, as some have, of becoming lazy with *Hairway* is wide of the mark. If anything, they were working harder than ever.

Yet some spark was, if not entirely missing, then slightly dimmer than before. *Hairway* is still a great record, or – to be picky – half a great record, with a bunch of more-than-adequate filler. It's an enjoyable listen, for hardcore fans and the new college rock and indie crowd alike. But it lacks the disagreeable intensity of *Locust Abortion Technician* and *Rembrandt Pussyhorse*, while being less of a full-on punk party record than their debut. On *Hairway*, the band are writing songs again, and with greater craft and consistency than ever before. That had to be progress, of a sort. But in the famous phrase of Vladimir Lenin, did one step forward mean two steps back?

Someone who was definitely still a fan of the band was actor-director Alex Winter, who approached them to star in a home-made film entitled *Bar-B-Que Movie*. Shot on hand-held Super 8 and just 11 minutes long, this underground short-short was ostensibly a parody of *The Texas Chainsaw Massacre*. The Buttholes, naturally enough, play the inbred cannibal family who waylay a vacationing couple, kidnap them and spike them with hallucinogens. They then murder their son and serve him up for dinner, before the film turns into a staged rendition of a Butthole Surfers live show.

At this point Winter was a film school graduate and budding auteur who had directed music videos as well as playing small parts in Hollywood films like *The Lost Boys*. But the following year he would become ever-recognisable as Bill S Preston Esquire, playing opposite Keanu Reeves as Ted 'Theodore' Logan in *Bill & Ted's Excellent Adventure*. At the same time as directing *Bar-B-Que Movie*, Winter and his regular writing partner Tom Stern collaborated with Gibby Haynes on the script for a demented gonzo horror movie to be called *Hideous Mutant Freekz*. Pitched as "*Beach Blanket Bingo* meets *The Evil Dead*", the film was envisaged as a full-length film vehicle for the

Buttholes Surfers, albeit a trashy, low-budget production that could be put together for around a hundred thousand dollars. But when no studio picked up on the idea, the script was completely rewritten, with the Butthole Surfers and most of the horror completely written out. Redeveloped as a surreal comedy, it was eventually picked up by Twentieth Century Fox and went into troubled production, finally emerging in 1993 as the compromised, cultish flop *Freaked*. One of the more bizarre offerings to be released (albeit furtively) by a major Hollywood studio, this tale of mutated sideshow freaks who rise up against their oppressors starred Winter alongside Randy Quaid, Mr T and Brooke Shields. The Butthole Surfers would still feature on the soundtrack, contributing 'Sweat Loaf' and 'Butter Queen,' while Paul Leary added 'Gumby Jack Flash'.

Bar-B-Que Movie (also known as *Entering Texas*) stars the future Academy Award-winning actor John Hawkes as Jerry, the archetypal 1950s-style straight nerd, a bumbling tourist off on a Texan vacation with his wife and young son, Jerry Jr. After an encounter with a violent hobo on the crazy golf course they follow signs for a "family style barbecue" and end up at the backwoods hillbilly home of the Butthole Surfers, playing themselves as inbred homicidal maniacs. While Teresa watches a loop of the exploding head scene from Cronenberg's *Scanners* on a portable TV set, Gibby pulls down his pants to add his "special grease" to the frying pan, which spells out the word 'Satan'.

Jerry Jr. has run off to explore, but the couple are both given a drink, which may also contain Gibby's "special grease" and which certainly has a powerful impact on Jerry, akin to both a hallucinogenic and a powerful amphetamine. After a barbecued Jerry Jr. is served up to him on a plate he gnaws off a great hunk of meat then runs off to find his son. Instead he stumbles into a vast, smoke-filled auditorium where he is mysteriously bound in cellophane and forced to watch as the Buttholes manifest demonically on stage and launch into 'Fast' with full depraved theatrics. Jerry then comes round in an outdoor cage, opposite his wife, where he is served another helping of his barbecued son.

The home movie comes over as much like *The Rocky Horror Show* in Hell as *The Texas Chainsaw Massacre,* while the moderate violence owes more to Tex Avery cartoons than any slasher gore fests. Most importantly, it captures the essence of the Butthole Surfers' appeal far more accurately then any of their later, major label-sponsored music videos ever would. But it also marks the point at which the Buttholes' itinerant lifestyle, drug-crazed madness and taboo-breaking art became fixed as mythology, rather than reality. The truth was, this version of the Butthole Surfers was already in the past; a past that to some extent could be recreated on film and on stage, but which was nevertheless already a part of musical history.

8
WEED FOR WEASELS

By the end of 1988 the Butthole Surfers were one of the most successful independent bands around, and the scene as a whole was approaching critical mass. REM had been the first to break through into the mainstream, and up in the Pacific North-West a little label called Sub Pop was creating quite a stir with bands like Mudhoney and its latest signings, an angsty three-piece known as Nirvana. Meanwhile, the Surfers were still touring constantly, selling out shows wherever they went, and commanding a staggering ten-to-fifteen thousand dollars per performance – though much of this went back into their touring budget, paying for their ever-more impressive barrage of lights, projections and theatrics. Unsurprisingly, they were being courted by several major labels and, feeling that they'd already outgrown Touch And Go, were seriously considering all offers.

September 1988 found the band back in Europe, where they recorded 'Blindman', 'Edgar' and 'Nee Nee' at a studio session for the John Peel Show on BBC Radio One, and played a headlining show at the Brixton Academy, supported by a somewhat miscast Primal Scream. Teresa lost her passport in London and missed several shows on the continent as a result, while this mini-tour also turned out to be Kathleen's final sortie as the band's regular dancer. She did join them one last time when they played at New York's Ritz on November 19, but otherwise she was focused on her new band, Beme Seed. Featuring Kathleen on lead vocals, this exemplary New York based freak-fuzz outfit went on to release three fine albums, starting with 1989's *The Future Is Attacking*. The Buttholes gave them a leg up when Beme Seed supported them in Atlanta on November 26.

The constant touring, onstage improvisation and the playing of many unrecorded songs in constantly changing sets – not to mention their loyal army of freaky fans – led many to compare the Butthole Surfers to the eighties equivalent of the Grateful Dead. And like the Dead, their legendary status in the underground was shored up by the massive proliferation of bootleg cassettes of their live shows, often of wildly varying quality. It was in response to this vast unofficial back catalogue that the band released an "official bootleg", the *Double Live* album, on their newly-founded Latino Buggerveil label in May 1989. The 2-LP set featured recordings from various shows over the previous year; ten bonus tracks on the CD and cassette were all drawn from a January 1987 show at the Theatre Gallery in Dallas, originally intended for a live split LP with Stickmen With Rayguns.

It might be a coincidence, but the release of *Double Live* seemed to mark the point where the Buttholes live show ceased to develop. The recordings captured them onstage at their peak, but now there was nowhere else for them to go. They were selling out the same venues every time they toured the states – the biggest venues that an underground band like the Butthole Surfers could reasonably expect to play, at that time.

Worse, the spontaneous, life-threatening chaos they were known for was now starting to seem just a little bit choreographed. In most cases, the band's reputation preceded them, and audiences knew what they were in for. There would be sick films and smoke; there would be noise and electronic effects and semi-synchronised high kicks during 'Sweat Loaf.' There would be strobe lights and body paint, and at a certain point Gibby would set the cymbals on fire. Was it all inevitably becoming a tad predictable?

Not that the band didn't still try to up the ante – but, other than some kind of live self-immolation, how could they top what they'd already achieved? Gibby began hoisting a shotgun on stage and firing blanks over the heads of the crowd, which was a kick for a while. But the wild post-punk era, when bands like the Buttholes genuinely existed on the outside of society and, like western pioneers, carved out their own lawless, dangerous kind of freedom, was coming to an end.

Just as the major record corporations had moved in on the psychedelic underground after Woodstock, so by the end of the eighties the likes of Sony, Warner Brothers and EMI could see that there was a massive potential audience for post-punk music, out in the suburbs and on the college campuses. It just had to be packaged right, with the rebelliousness and political radicalism smoothed down and made palatable and safe, while still retaining just enough edge and attitude to give the kids a frisson of excitement. It would be marketed as alternative rock, college rock or, most ironically of all, indie rock. But, most importantly, it would all be rock music, and, despite generational quirks, the A&R and publicity departments were determined that it would essentially be no different to Led Zeppelin, Pink Floyd, the Rolling Stones or any of the other aging cash cows that the industry urgently needed to replace.

Another sign of the times came when Teresa Nervosa quit the band for the second time that summer, just prior to another trip to the UK and an appearance third on the bill on the main stage at that year's Reading Rock Festival. "I had developed a really big fear of flying," Teresa later said. "I always thought the plane was going to crash. I couldn't figure out what was wrong with me. I didn't want to leave the band, but I really wasn't well, I was flipping out, drinking too much and all that."

After leaving the band, Teresa suffered from seizures and depression, and in 1993 had brain surgery for an aneurysm. Despite famously appearing as 'Pap Smear Pusher' in Richard Linklater's generation-defining, Austin-set cult movie *Slackers* in 1991, it took nearly 20 years for Teresa Taylor to recover and begin living a normal life again.

The Butthole Surfers' first recording as a four-piece was also their last for Touch And Go in the US, and Blast First in the UK. The *Widowermaker* EP was released in September 1989, as a stateside 12-inch and a 10-inch in Britain. As with the *Cream Corn From The Socket Of Davis* EP, track titles were changed according to country;

the song America knew as 'The Colored FBI Guy' was known in Britain as '1401' (the title that had always appeared on band set lists).

Again, the record was an enjoyable enough listen, while breaking no new ground. 'The Bong Song' was a twisted stoner nugget, with processed acoustic guitar, slabs of noise and glistening keyboards combining with appropriate coughing and retching effects as Gibby rambled on about "disarray cowboys with weed for our weasels" and "illicit vibrations encoded with light rays." '1401' was a moody ballad undercut, as ever, by Gibby's creepy vocal and Paul's wayward guitar solo. 'Booze Tobacco Dope Pussy Cars' though was almost a parody of what an outsider might think the Butthole Surfers were all about. A punk-metal redneck frat anthem, it simultaneously harked back to their hardcore beginnings and looked forward to Gibby's hit collaboration with Ministry, 'Jesus Built My Hotrod'.

Best was the pounding 'Helicopter', a down and dirty grebo stomp riding another driving, Sabbath-influenced bass line that eventually breaks up into a Gary-Glitter-in-dub finale, crying out for the old King and Teresa double-drumming team. "Preacher, don't touch me! Doctor, don't touch me there!" Gibby howls, demanding freedom from all authority: social, spiritual, mental and physical. Death itself shall have no damn dominion over this boy.

By far the biggest band on Touch And Go, the Butthole Surfers were convinced that the little label just didn't have the resources to properly promote them, let alone push the band to the next level. Despite their growing status and increased draw as a live act, their albums were still selling a maximum 100,000 copies, which seemed to be the limit of the label's distribution network. And while many thought it amusingly incongruous that Paul and Gibby were business majors, they always had one eye on the bottom line. They were determined to do whatever it took, not only to survive but to grow, and to maximise their profits. This wasn't a sell-out mentality; they never claimed to be idealists in the first place. "We had to claw and fight for everything," Leary would claim. "That's what punk rock was about anyway. It's not about causes or right and wrong. It's about fighting."

The split with Touch And Go – and Blast First in the UK – was relatively amicable, at least initially. In the case of the latter label,

Gibby even showed up unannounced at the door of label head Paul Smith – then living in New York – and told him, "We're going to go out and get fucked," before taking the Englishman on a two-week bender. None of the major labels that came calling could offer a satisfactory deal however, so the band ended up signing a short-term contract with the largest indie label that was interested: the London based Rough Trade.

It's tempting to wonder if the band already had the Capitol deal lined up when they jumped to Rough Trade, and used the indie label as a stepping stone to the major leagues. Rough Trade apparently paid them a ridiculous amount of money upfront, for what amounted to three albums in two years – one by the Buttholes, and two side projects that were never going to be particularly lucrative. The label's success was built largely on the Smiths, who had disbanded in 1987, but Rough Trade was also an international distributor handling the accounts of many smaller labels, and was big enough to have branches in America and Europe. Unfortunately, and presumably unbeknownst to the band, at the time the Buttholes signed the label was already in financial difficulties, with Rough Trade America in particular suffering serious cash flow problems.

Nevertheless, early signs were promising. The first Butthole Surfers release on Rough Trade wasn't actually by the band at all, but by the Jackofficers – who for this release were a duo of Gibby and Jeff, though the name, at least, had existed for far longer. It's on record that in 1984 the band had played an Austin bar show as the Jackofficers, in which Gibby was "born" onto the stage via a bloody mattress while the band played, augmented by synthesisers. A performance art element involved Scratch Acid singer David Yow acting drunk and belligerent all night, coming up to Gibby between songs and shouting "you owe me money," and "where's my two bucks, motherfucker?" while spitting on him. Towards the end of the set Yow smashed a fake wine bottle over Gibby's head, Gibby feigned collapse and Yow took over lead vocal on a cover of Scratch Acid's 'Cannibal'.

"But we fucked it up totally," Gibby recalled, "and they all thought this was a real bottle fight. And this one guy stepped out of the audience and punched Yow right in the face."

"Blood's spewing everywhere and people started fighting with each other," remembered audience member Brent Grulke. "The aggression level in that place was phenomenal. No-one knew it was staged. It was brilliant."

Two years later, Jeff Pinkus's first show with the band was actually as a member of the Jackofficers. In another example of their subterranean business acumen, Gibby and Paul had figured out that they could make more money by being their own support band. Thus at Jeff's first show, on January 10 1986, the Jackofficers were the Buttholes' opening act: the guys came out with contact mics down their pants, which they would whack on to trigger samples. Jackofficers t-shirts had also been available for at least three years, and the *Digital Dump* recordings had been used as a concert intro tape for at least a year before the album came out.

Actually, while definitely reflecting the early house music and hip-hop sounds of the time, *Digital Dump* has aged remarkably well. Tracks like the appropriately named 'Time Machines' parts one and two reflect the pre-internet era when musical sampling seemed almost like a form of magic, a way of combining evocative audio snippets of past times and different cultures in a hyper-modern context, and so creating for a few minutes the illusion of an entirely new reality.

This approach had its roots in the literary and artistic cut-ups of William Burroughs and Brion Gysin, while early industrial outsider artists like Coil and Throbbing Gristle applied their discoveries and techniques to experimental music. Composed entirely of programmed drum machine beats and samples, *Digital Dump* explicitly makes the connection between these pioneers and the dance-based electronic music that was the soundtrack to a new psychedelic generation, coming of age in techno clubs and massive outdoor raves.

There's more than a touch of typical Buttholes madness to a track like 'Swinger's Club', but overall the album has a surprising lightness of touch, gliding rather than pummelling, an ever-unfolding collage that nevertheless retains a pleasing DIY rawness when compared to the far more successful, but not entirely dissimilar, debut album by the Orb, that came out a full year later. The aforementioned 'Time Machines' juxtaposes dialogue from the Iran-Contra hearings with some of the most over-used samples of dance music at the time, to hugely entertaining effect; '#6' utilises dialogue from cult sixties TV show *The Prisoner* alongside a disapproving English broadcaster referring to "long-haired, drug-crazed hippies."

There are similarities to the early eighties albums of Cabaret Voltaire and the mid-period work of former Butthole Surfers support act the Shamen, as well as the experiments with dance music that Psychic TV were making at the time. 'An Hawaiian Christmas Song' has some of the understated eeriness of the Residents, while even closing track 'Flush' – a treated sample of a flushing toilet – has a sonic appeal that goes beyond its punk-Dada lame joke status. The Jackofficers went on to tour the album in Europe, with a naked Kathleen Lynch re-joining Gibby and Jeff onstage, presumably to provide some visual entertainment while the boys just pressed play on their samplers or mugged to the crowd with a bass synth.

The Butthole Surfers returned with an astonishing version of the 13th Floor Elevators' 'Earthquake', recorded for a Roky Erickson tribute album, *Where The Pyramid Meets The Eye,* released on Halloween 1990. The album was also a fundraiser for Erickson's legal and medical bills, and boasted an impressive line-up, including the Jesus And Mary Chain, ZZ Top, REM, Primal Scream and Julian Cope. The Buttholes' supercharged cover stands out, however, for remaining respectfully faithful to the original, while adding a whole new level of Texan dementia; their love for the song bleeds through in every unstable note.

In December, the Butthole Surfers returned with their first single-proper – as opposed to a standalone EP – a cover of Donovan's 'Hurdy Gurdy Man', which they had played live during 1984 and 1985, but never since. Recording the track at this late stage was a clear bid for commercial breakthrough, and with the greater muscle of Rough Trade America behind them, the single came out in multiple formats and with an MTV-ready video clip for the title track. But although the record gained a significant amount of airplay, it failed to chart. The parent album, *Piouhgd*, followed in February 1991.

Sometimes mistakenly spelt "*Pioughd*," even on the spine of the later Capitol Records reissue, the album title was a nonsense word invented by the band, and intended to be unpronounceable. However, Rough Trade issued a press release claiming the word should be pronounced "pee-oh-d", as in P.O.'d, or pissed off. In interviews, Gibby sometimes claimed that it was a Navajo Indian code word meaning "I told you so", before withdrawing this explanation and saying that actually he just hit some random keys on the typewriter.

Opinions of this record have divided fans and critics, and the band themselves all but disowned it within a couple of years of the album's release. "It was a joke on Rough Trade," Gibby claimed at the beginning of 1993, with Paul putting the record's faults down to the fact that the band recorded it in their bathroom, and saying that he'd rather see it dumped in the garbage than reissued. Nevertheless, the LP does have its supporters, with many fans seeing it as the last example of the old-style Buttholes before their major label makeover, and others seeing it as a transitional record, bridging the two eras.

The album opens with the two-part 'Revolution'. The first part is a grungy, stoner rock jam with howling, wordless vocals overlaid with echo and other effects. This gives way to strummed acoustic guitar and multi-tracked Gibby vocals, in what seems to be a satire on the supposed radicalism of turn-of-the-decade alternative rock. "We're gonna have a revolution and we don't even know why," Gibby sings. But after what's a relatively conventional fuzz-guitar solo by Buttholes standards, he turns the tables: "In these times of counter-revolution, you're gonna encounter a counter-revolutionary man," before the whole thing devolves into repeated chants of "Garry Shandling, Garry Shandling."

"He's just one of those people that haunt me," Gibby would explain when asked why the comedian's name was used. He also bemoaned the fact that Rough Trade delayed the album's release for so long that *It's Garry Shandling's Show* had been axed by the time it came out. At the risk of taking the song too seriously, we must ask; is Garry Shandling the counter-revolutionary man previously mentioned? What of the other celebrity names (Helen Hunt, Jodie Foster) that crop up as the song winds towards its climax, with sirens wailing, telephones ringing and plastic synthesised strings sawing away?

'Lonesome Bulldog' is probably the most annoying song on the album, a joke country and western number featuring banjo and clip-clop horse's hooves/coconut shell percussion. Leary delivers the spoken word vocal in a bizarre attempt at an Australian accent, telling the story of Mahatma Gandhi, "a little spindly-bottomed, raggedy-headed boy that grew up in a Western Kentucky village called Johnsonville, in Harrison County, where he grew up." His mother was a white woman, his father a Rastafarian, "who refused to buy the family seafood on their outings," and so on.

The surreal, childishly obscene humour is very much in the vein of John Kricfalusi's original *Ren And Stimpy Show*, which premiered six months after *Piouhgd* was released. It's funny enough on first hearing, but it goes on far too long, which may be the point. There's an accordion solo; then a flute solo (both possibly synthesised), and when the song finally ends- it starts again! Three more times in fact, with Lonesome Bulldog parts II-IV scattered throughout the rest of the album, each a brief instrumental reprise of the theme with Leary's electric guitar solo growing more warped and drunk-sounding each time around.

'The Hurdy Gurdy Man' is a surprisingly faithful cover of the Donovan original that sidelines the twee hippy sentiment and foregrounds the drug-damaged creepiness. Leary's vocals shimmer and wobble in dislocated fashion, while his guitar solo dips and cuts like a shell-shocked gravedigger decomposing in the acid rain, or limps across the ultra-violet sky like a haemorrhaging seagull. The song may have been a diluted rendering of the Buttholes' former craziness, but that dilution allowed it to get onto mainstream radio and MTV, where it sounded all the weirder in context. Furthermore, the track sounded great on the speed-and-strychnine-spiked LSD of the early nineties, and fitted perfectly with the bastardised, re-mixed sixties revival happening in music at the time; a pseudo-psychedelic vibe that wrapped hedonistic, ecstasy-fuelled rave culture round post-punk guitar rock and cast it all in a borrowed paisley haze.

The rather formless guitar and organ garage stomp of 'Golden Showers' features Gibby back on rasping saxophone, while 'Blindman' is a classic Buttholes grind, Stooges- and Cramps-influenced hard rock with unintelligible vocals that speed up nightmarishly and then seem to swallow themselves. And 'No, I'm Iron Man' – a noise jam with added Gibbytronix – is not so much another Black Sabbath pastiche as a tribute to the band's loyal fans on the Atlanta drag scene.

Presumably because they could and it seemed funny at the time, the band resurrected the lyrics to 'Something' from their first EP and set them to the tune of the Jesus and Mary Chain's 'Never Understand', complete with "uh huh" vocal hooks and screaming / feedback solo that almost outdoes the original. And the album ends with 'P.S.Y.', a song which the band had played live in various forms for years, usually under the title 'Psychedelic Jam'. There's been much speculation about what the letters stand for, with some suggesting that it's a reference to Sonic Youth. As far as I can see though, it's just a contraction of 'psychedelic' and doesn't actually stand for anything.

Certainly Gibby's introductory droning vocals seem to be describing the beginnings of an acid trip: "Here we go – all I see inside my head is gentle silent secret show, with shifting walls of blinding light." Then the metal-raga guitars take off into a nightmare universe of broken perspectives and fleeting kaleidoscopic beauty. Eventually it shifts into a driving Velvet Underground-type narrative about runaways, drugs, shotgun deaths and Nikki, who was in the KKK, and Lisa, who was a Nazi too. Finally it shifts again into a stomping, howling finale.

It may not be the equal of *Hairway To Steven*, and it certainly isn't *Locust Abortion Technician*, but *Piouhgd* isn't at all bad either. It kind of all hinges on how far you can tolerate the Lonesome Bulldog sequence, which must be intended as a deliberate endurance test. That song aside, it's a solid, deranged, funny and sometimes scary album. Certainly 'Blindman', 'P.S.Y.' and arguably 'The Hurdy Gurdy Man' can stand with the Butthole Surfers' finest moments – though perhaps tellingly, they're also the oldest songs chosen for the record. Don't write off *Piouhgd* as a mess; okay, it is a bit of a mess, but it's a glorious one. And the Butthole Surfers never claimed to be consistent, after all.

9
CLEAN IT UP

March 1991 saw the band travel to Australia and New Zealand for the first time, and back in the States that summer they joined the inaugural Lollapalooza tour, appearing alongside Jane's Addiction, Siouxsie and the Banshees, Living Colour, Nine Inch Nails, Ice-T and the Rollins Band. Conceived by Jane's Addiction singer Perry Farrell as a multi-media, cross-genre travelling circus tour representing the entire "alternative nation", Lollapalooza was a major step up for the Butthole Surfers. For all Farrell's idealistic motives, the tour was very different to the DIY, underground punk club circuit the band had ground around throughout the 1980s. Now, the Buttholes were playing mainly to wholesome suburban teens who had discovered the alternative culture through shopping malls and MTV. Lollapalooza would come to represent the commodification of post-punk and alternative culture, and though that first tour was still a relatively fresh and edgy proposition for its audience, the Buttholes were coming at it from the other end. For them it was a toehold in the mainstream corporate culture that they were determined to infiltrate, like a tapeworm entering its host.

"Lollapalooza was the first tour where we didn't have to drive our own vehicle, set up our own equipment, tune our own guitars, and collect our own money at the end," Paul Leary remembered. "That set us free, so we could get a little bit fucked up." The band generally played in the afternoon, giving them plenty of time to hang out and get wasted. They had their own tour bus and plenty of complimentary beer and liquor. The Buttholes' bus became the place to hang out and get stoned for bigger acts who didn't want to be found, while the band found that travelling in a big rock star tour bus granted them a certain level of immunity from the cops.

"Cops think like Willie Nelson's on the bus with a bunch of naked chicks," Gibby recalled. "They won't step in there, it's holy ground."

Yet Lollapalooza also marked the end of the Butthole Surfers' ten-year communal lifestyle. "We made a bunch of money and I guess it was instrumental in getting to live like normal people do," Paul noted. In Leary's case, that meant moving out of the ranch commune to get married. King had already quietly got his own place in Austin, and Jeff and Gibby soon moved into separate homes too.

King invested his time and money in starting his own record label, Trance Syndicate, in 1990. "It was my New Year's resolution to start a record label," he said. "By then I had the resources to pull it off, so I challenged myself. If I was just playing drums for fifteen years, I'd be incredibly boring. I like to think I'm not that boring." Initial signings included Crust, Pain Teens, Ed Hall and Coffey's own experimental electronic band Drain, which saw him reunited with Hugh Beaumont Experience bass player David McCreath.

Paul Leary released his solo album, *The History of Dogs*, through Rough Trade in April 1991. "It sucks," Paul told *Fiz* magazine in January 1993, though as usual he was being unnecessarily self-critical. Combining dumbed-down punk-metal guitars with synthesisers and a pounding drum machine beat, at times the LP sounds like a more lo-fi cousin of roughly contemporary albums by the Jesus and Mary Chain (*Automatic*) or the Sisters of Mercy (*Vision Thing*). There's also a hint of the high-gloss, metronomic take on Texas boogie that ZZ Top trademarked on 1983's *Eliminator*. It's pulled into the realms of the bizarre by Leary's vocals, shifting from a stoned falsetto to a sinister, subterranean growl swathed in reverb, and also his elliptical, paranoid lyrics, which conjure pictures of him staying up all night watching several news channels at once, stockpiling tinned goods and barricading the door against nuclear Armageddon or social and environmental collapse.

For once, the description 'solo album' means exactly that: Leary plays and produces everything. The result sounds isolated and claustrophobic, like you're stuck inside the man's head. There are none of the expansive, wigged-out solos you associate with his playing on Butthole Surfers albums, just tight squalls of screeching licks, wrenched into place. It circles itself, locked into the same groove, as though designed to be played on a constant loop. Yet there's much to enjoy, from the ominous synth and acoustic guitar arpeggios of 'The Birds Are Dying' to the chugging, nervous tension hard rock of 'Apollo One' ("A little sparky has lit up the oxygen").

Things get even weirder on the faux-wardance of 'Indians Storm The Government' ("I don't know what the squashman thinks / His face is ink and his eyes don't blink") and the Bontempi waltz of 'Too Many People'.

'Is It Mikey' and 'The City' are enjoyably gothic and brooding, while closing ballad 'Fine Home' is actually quite moving, its valedictory sentiment ("The children of the night will find a way to make the new day") set to the kind of reverberating kick drums, tambourine and whistling (!) that usually accompany Christmas number ones.

While Paul was locked in the studio creating his oblique, hermetic solo statement, Gibby co-wrote and sang vocals on what would become Chicago industrial maniacs Ministry's best-known song, 'Jesus Built My Hotrod', released as a single in November 1991. "Jesus Built My Hotrod came about, I think, at Lollapalooza," Gibby told *Penny Black Music*. "They had that killer riff, and the guitar solo, but they didn't really know what to do with it, so I said I'd help them make something of it. I did the vocals in one take. Well, I tried to do a couple of other takes, but they didn't really turn out that good, so we had to use the first one."

"Gibby came down completely drunk off his ass to the studio we're at in Chicago," Ministry's Al Jourgensen later claimed. "He couldn't even sit on a stool, let alone sing. I mean, he was wasted. He fell off the stool about ten times during the recording of that vocal. He made no sense and it was just gibberish. So I spent two weeks editing tape of what he did."

Many feel that Gibby's descent into serious drug abuse began around the time of his collaboration with Ministry, whose leader Al Jourgensen was a known heroin user. "This was when Ministry was thinking about moving to Austin and Gibby was working with Al Jourgensen and they did 'Jesus Built My Hotrod'," said journalist Margaret Moser. "It was around this time that Gibby got into heroin, and when he left the Ministry enclave in Chicago he slipped into smoking crack and doing heroin all the time."

"I was too fucked up – emotionally, chemically, economically," Gibby says. "The economic part was that I had too much money."

Too much money was not one of the problems afflicting the Buttholes' label, Rough Trade, though in a way the company was a victim of its own success. Founded in London by Geoff Travis in the late 1970s, Rough Trade was one of the original and iconic indie labels of the post-punk era. By 1991 it was an international business, and also a distribution network for many other independent labels. It retained an idealistic, anti-capitalist ethos that was increasingly at odds with the large-scale business dealings it was involved in, and soon found that it was in over its head. The American franchise, in particular, was continuing to struggle.

"I would pick up the phone to London and say, 'I think we've had our best month ever, we've just shipped X thousand records'," remembered Robin Hurley, who had taken over the San Francisco based Rough Trade Inc. in 1987. "Not realising that we might have to wait months to get paid. As our business grew, our cash flow became crippled."

Despite – or almost because of – achieving several top ten albums and singles over the turn of the decade, the problems were mounting. Tax problems, poor management and a growing list of worried creditors eventually led to the company going into receivership. Ironically, the company called in to audit and oversee the process of administration were the accountancy firm Peat Marwick – Gibby's old employers, from back in the days when he was Trinity University's Accounting Student of the Year.

When Rough Trade filed for bankruptcy at the end of 1991, the Butthole Surfers at least came out better than most, having retained the rights to their recordings, since they were made at their home studio in Driftwood. The rest of the label's back catalogue rights and masters were auctioned off to pay their debts. Though the Buttholes undoubtedly lost money, they were able to walk away relatively unscathed and straight into a new deal – with the major label Capitol.

Capitol President and CEO Hale Milgrim was a fan of the Grateful Dead who saw some similar qualities in the Buttholes, particularly in the way they constantly evolved and improvised on stage. Yet he was not without reservations concerning the group. "I knew that we would have some problems with key accounts that are unfortunately into censorship," he said. "I talked to the promotion department and said look, whatever you can get the group to go along with; the 'B-hole' Surfers would be appreciated. But I knew what I was signing."

Paul Leary recalled Hale Milgrim as "a cool dude. They hooked us up with John Paul Jones, but they didn't really know what to do with us at first, so we could do whatever we wanted." Moreover, the band, and Leary in particular, were just happy to be signed to the same label as their seventies heroes, Grand Funk Railroad.

The Butthole Surfers celebrated the news that they'd be working with John Paul Jones by briefly adding a cover of Led Zeppelin's 'Communication Breakdown' to their set over the New Year period, but the band spent the majority of 1992 off the road and in the studio. *Independent Worm Saloon* took two months to record, a relatively long time for the Butthole Surfers to spend on one album. Some of that time, admittedly, was spent goofing around, jamming on Led Zeppelin songs with "John motherfucking Paul motherfucking ass Jones," as Paul Leary excitedly referred to him in one interview. "We set up a keyboard for him and started jamming on 'Kashmir'," he went on, with King claiming that they warmed up every day with Gregorian chanting and "Dances to the Fairy Queen of the Lake."

"He was like a horrible drunk when we were doing that record, but we were loaded too," Gibby recalled, years later. "We spent so much money on that record! We basically spent a fortune to hang out with some guy from Led Zeppelin!"

Capitol released *Independent Worm Saloon* in March 1993. Many of the fans who'd accused the band of selling out for signing to

Capitol felt their contempt justified when they heard the finished album. *Saloon* was a slickly-produced, polished, pumped-up hard rock album seemingly sculpted with MTV in mind, and targeted at the suburban rebels who had bought 'Jesus Built My Hotrod' and made the song Ministry's biggest hit. Certainly, the high production values and layered sonic clarity are a shock to the system for any old-school Buttholes fan, and the album can certainly sound bombastic and repetitive by the end of its sixty-two minute duration. But essentially, *Independent Worm Saloon* is still the same wayward, twisted, chaotic and psychedelic Butthole Surfers – just with a whole lot more money and better quality toys to play with.

It opens with the band's first semi-hit single, 'Who Was In My Room Last Night'. Their long-standing love of Black Sabbath is more evident than ever on this track, and it sets the template for the whole album: gonzo rock workouts with a monomaniacal, robotic rhythm section and barely intelligible, gibbering lunatic vocals. It's punk and heavy metal meeting at their lowest common denominator and retooled with military-strength hardware. But when it works, as it often does, the results are exhilarating, and irresistible fun.

'Who Was in My Room…' begins with Gibby singing, in his most childlike and wispy voice, "I'm flying, I'm flying away…", like Peter Pan, flying in through Wendy's window and spiriting her away to Neverland, which – in the context of a creepy song about someone possibly coming into your room at night, and touching you while you're lying in bed – is somewhat disturbing. On the other hand, there are hints in the lyrics that the stranger is imaginary, or indeed that the stranger is the narrator himself.

"It took a little time, but I figured they were mine, there were fingers running down my chest." This existential reading of the song asks, who is the "I" that sleeps, and the "I" that dreams? If "I" am elsewhere in mental space, then who is the stranger that looks like me, the body lying in my bed? Am I my body, or is my body a stranger with whom I share the same space? Or is the song about the shadow self, the mysterious other, demon or angel, that so many artists have spoken about experiencing; the usually suppressed, subconscious right brain self that sometimes takes over in times of crisis?

'The Wooden Song' is a haunting folk-rock ballad, a surprisingly sincere-sounding break-up song with a spiralling electric guitar solo; 'Tongue' a Zappa-esque piece of prog-metal madness with several stylistic shifts. The comedy skit 'Chewin' Georges Lucas' Chocolate' segues into the driving punk-metal of 'Goofy's Concern', an obscenity-strewn rant about not giving a fuck that actually turns out to be a love song: "I don't give a fuck about what you do / All I ever fuckin' think about is you." It's kind of sweet.

The twisted, heavy lament 'Alcohol' could have sat happily on any Butthole Surfers album from the eighties, while 'Dog Inside Your Body', driven by trip-hammer industrial beats, is another twisted love song, about wanting to really get through to someone, kinks, perversions and all; actually, especially the kinks and perversions. "I'm tired of touching you; I want to cut on through." Cutting through their inhibitions and repressions won't be pretty however, and it will probably be painful; but it's the only way to get rid of "the dog inside your body, he's got you by the throat."

The heavy metal folk-rock of 'Strawberry' seems to be about grieving and coping with the premature death of someone close, while many have considered 'Some Dispute Over T-shirt Sales' to be a near-cover of 'Jesus Built My Hotrod', due to the similarity in the vocal delivery. Actually though the band had been playing the song live since 1990, when it was known as 'Watlo' – Paul Leary's nickname, based on the way his Mexican school friends would pronounce his surname of Walthall. And really, Gibby's trademark Texan wildcat preacher vocals are no more similar to his performance on 'Jesus Built My Hotrod' than they are to several earlier Buttholes songs.

'Dancing Fool' and 'You Don't Know Me' also date back to 1990 and 1989 respectively. The former is a Paul Leary tour de force, the guitarist hollering "Dance like cancer!" and "Fuck you, I'm the dancing fool!" over a veritable autobahn of punishing Wagnerian Panzer attack guitars, remorseless and unstoppable. The latter seems to be Gibby's riposte to the fans who accuse the band of selling out their punk-acid roots, or possibly to bitchy music journalists peddling a shallow, surface interpretation of the band's work. "You don't know me, you just know my name / You want to see me ruined, I know that's your game / Taking tips instead of reading rhymes / You want to take a tip and redefine your mind."

'The Annoying Song' has Gibby's vocals sped up to near-unintelligible helium pitch, sounding like some evil baby space alien chanting over solid steel walls of polished metal guitars. The crunching 'Dust Devil' may be the best song ever about a hand-held vacuum cleaner with "the power of an upright," while 'Leave Me Alone' and 'Edgar' (finally committed to record after debuting on that 1988 Peel session) are both layered Leary guitar jams in excelsis. 'The Ballad of Naked Man' meanwhile, featuring John Paul Jones on bass alongside banjo and acoustic guitar, was apparently about an actual naked man who would walk past the studio window at the same time every day.

The album ends with an all-time Butthole Surfers freak-out classic, the near-nine minutes of 'Clean It Up'. Any casual listeners who can make it through the opening two minutes of exaggerated vomiting sounds and bowel-twitching bass are then hurled into the sound of a blistering guitar duel between Paul Leary and guest Helios Creed of Chrome, whose dying-star howl reverberates across the rhythm section's apocalyptic black hole rumble. This is not the sound of a band that have sold out and cleaned up their act, that's for sure. Nothing else on a major label in the 1990s got as far out and psychedelic as this track.

Nevertheless, *Independent Worm Saloon* was still the hit the band and their label needed it to be. The video for 'Who Was In My Room Last Night' found itself on permanent rotation on MTV that spring, and the single reached number 24 on the Alternative Rock Charts. The band spent the whole summer on a massive co-headlining tour with Stone Temple Pilots, before returning to the UK for the 1993 Reading Festival, and then embarked on a short tour of Japan with Boredoms. A December US tour with the Mighty Mighty Bosstones was cancelled when the latter band pulled out, but the Buttholes made up for it with a mini-stadium tour over the New Year period opening for Nirvana. Unfortunately, these dates would mark the end of Jeff Pinkus's tenure with the band.

The true reason for Pinkus's sudden departure is unknown, although the blanket term "personal and creative differences" seems to cover it. Certainly it had been a long, strange ride for Pinkus, who was only 17 when he joined the band, and later claimed that he never intended it to be permanent. It's possible that he realised sooner than the others that being on a major label wasn't an entirely agreeable experience, but there's no doubt too that Gibby's increasing reliance on heroin was a factor in him quitting.

"It was life threatening," says Paul Leary of Gibby's drug problems, pointing out that even though the band was in a position where they could control their own destiny, had access to top of the range studios and the support of an international record label, suddenly everything seemed to be falling apart. "We lost our bass player... what Gibby was doing to himself was so depressing I couldn't get out of bed."

"He'd walk into the Black Cat bar and his eyes were going in two different directions," recalled Margaret Moser. "He smelled bad. He had that translucent look, like he didn't know what was going on."

Heroin and other hard drug use had become almost endemic among the post-grunge alternative community by the early nineties. Many of the former underground musicians who had become stars used the drug to shore up their self-esteem and to fight their growing alienation from the corporate culture into which they'd become absorbed. Haynes finally went into rehab at LA's Exodus Recovery Center in early 1994, and coincidentally ended up sharing a room with Kurt Cobain. The troubled Nirvana frontman was reaching the end of his own losing battle with heroin addiction, and Gibby was one of the last people to see him alive. Cobain climbed the facility fence on March 31 and was found dead at his Seattle home eight days later.

On leaving rehab, Gibby needed money and began hosting a morning show on Austin's then-new alternative rock radio station KROX-FM, AKA 101X. He'd wanted to do a morning show because his dad had always hosted his Mr Peppermint TV show on Saturday morning. It also meant that he would discipline himself to go to bed early the night before, and would be sober on air. Unfortunately, after they'd milked the situation for publicity, the station decided that Gibby's style wasn't quite suitable for the morning show and shifted his time slot to nine in the evening.

The change was a disaster, as going out in the evening for Gibby inevitably meant loading up on drink and drugs. "I called the station the first night and I was like, do you want me to go down there? I mean, he's falling apart, just listen to him," Gibby's father, Jerry Haynes, recalled. "One night he just locked the engineer out and then just rambled for two hours and didn't even do an air call, it was hysterical. He had Mike Watt on the phone and he wouldn't let him go. I think the band getting back together saved him more than anything, not AA."

After 'Who Was In My Room Last Night' had proved to be a radio and video hit, Capitol were determined to maximise their investment in the Butthole Surfers, despite the fact that the band seemed to be falling apart. "It was just a matter of making the record that would make a difference in their career rather than another Butthole Surfers mind-fuck that would appeal to a limited audience," said Capitol vice-president Tim Devine, who started working with the band after *Independent Worm Saloon*. "I knew that after 12 years they had enough base and were ready for the big time."

What the band weren't ready for yet though was to make another album; indeed, with Jeff gone and Gibby strung out, and King focussed on running Trance Syndicate, there barely was a band. To keep their profile up, Devine tirelessly licensed Buttholes tracks to film soundtracks, video games and even a Nintendo commercial. He also hooked Gibby up with actor Johnny Depp (who was a big fan of 'Jesus Built My Hotrod'), Flea from the Chilli Peppers, Steve Jones from the Sex Pistols and Andrew Weiss from Ween to form the band P. Their sole album was conceived purely as a device to keep the Butthole Surfers' visibility up, and was a loss leader in terms of sales – though the band did score a fluke number one single in South East Asia with their cover of Abba's 'Dancing Queen'.

The project also saw Gibby sucked further into the celebrity Hollywood lifestyle, with all of its attendant vices. P was playing at LA's Viper Room club the night that River Phoenix fatally overdosed on a combination of heroin and cocaine. The young actor had become a good friend of Gibby's. "We were playing a song and River Phoenix was right down in front of me," the singer recalled. "We started the song 'Michael Stipe' and it's got River's name in it. So we were singing up on stage and right at that moment he was basically on the sidewalk.

CLEAN IT UP

I saw him right at the beginning of the song, then I didn't see River anymore. I've got a guitar solo, and at the end of the guitar solo, Johnny stepped off stage. He was frightened. River died just a few feet away from us, right on the other side of the wall."

10

YOU ALWAYS END
UP WASTED

The Whole Truth… And Nothing Butt was originally a 1994 bootleg album put out as a CD by Totonka Records. It consisted of live tracks recorded at various different shows, two songs from the band's 1983 demo tape, and a 1987 radio interview. When King Coffey came across it he liked it enough to put it out himself on Trance Syndicate in 1995.

The demo tracks open the album: versions of 'Butthole Surfer' and 'Something' that immediately predate *Brown Reason to Live*. Four songs from a September 1985 concert at San Antonio's Cameo Theatre give a rare chance to hear just how solid the elusive Juan Molina was on bass, while Jeff Pinkus is on board for the three numbers taped at San Francisco's Mabuhay Gardens in January the following year. The remaining seven live tracks date from 1988-1993, so that the album essentially shows how the Butthole Surfers changed and grew over a ten-year period. A hilarious interview from New York's WYNU gives context and rounds out the release.

The Whole Truth… was immediately preceded on Trance Syndicate by *All That May Do My Rhyme*, the first new album in over a decade by the troubled former 13th Floor Elevators singer Roky Erickson. This was a true labour of love by Coffey, who had befriended Roky and essentially became his main confidant and carer during this period. Paul Leary, who played guitar on three tracks on the album, recalled Roky as one of the few characters who could out-weird the Butthole Surfers. "He came into the studio with an aluminium foil hat," he recalls. "Stuart [Sullivan engineer] asked what it was for and Roky told him it was to keep the rays off of his head. Stuart told him the studio was lead-lined, so Roky took the hat off. Roky came over to our house one time. We had just decorated our bathroom with fluorescent paint and stuff. He went in there and didn't come out for forty-five minutes. We gave him a pickled bat in a jar, and he wouldn't stop staring at it."

In another link back to the psychedelic icons of the 1960s, Gibby spent a brief period in the mid-nineties crashing at the home of the legendary counter-culture figurehead, acid guru, psychologist and futurologist Timothy Leary. According to Al Jourgensen's 2015 autobiography, *Ministry: The Lost Gospels,* for a while Gibby and Jourgensen acted as drug guinea pigs for Leary, happily testing out new chemical concoctions while the eminent doctor took notes on the effects. In the book, Haynes recalls waking up in Leary's study with Leary furiously typing up notes just three feet away. Gibby's penis was hanging out of his trousers and was "warm and moist". He dimly remembered pissing in Leary's kitchen, but reasoned it was Leary's fault as he shouldn't have had a kitchen that was entirely white; to Gibby, the white room is always the bathroom, as another couple who briefly hosted him, who had an all-white bedroom, found out at their expense. Gibby also admitted that he let Leary's blind dog shit on the carpet, while Jourgensen recalled that Leary finally kicked Gibby out after he urinated in the drawer of an antique desk in that same study.

By this time Hale Milgrim had moved on from Capitol and Gary Gersh was the new company president. Gersh was famous for being the man who signed Nirvana to Geffen, and was supposed to have an affinity with the nineties 'alt-rock' phenomenon that bewildered many of his corporate peers. But the Butthole Surfers' relationship with Gersh was somewhat strained.

"Gary kind of freaked me out," Paul Leary admitted. "I remember him calling us to his office to celebrate our album going gold. He came up to me and said 'Hi, I'm Gary Gersh. I just want you to know that

I really respect what you do.' About five minutes later he came up to me again and said 'Hi, I'm Gary Gersh. I just want you to know that I really respect what you do.'"

Capitol hooked the band up with producer Steve Thompson, and together they spent eight weeks in Todd Rungren's Bearsville studio in upstate New York recording the new album. Thompson was happy with the results, but the band felt that more work needed to be done and re-recorded several tracks with Leary producing, as well as adding three or four new songs. Everyone was impressed with Leary's indomitable work ethic in the face of all adversity, as well as his unwavering commitment to making brilliant but deliberately stupid rock music.

The label knew they were onto a winner with the album, and pulled out all the stops in terms of promotion. It was obviously the most commercial thing the Butthole Surfers had ever done, and arguably band and record company both realised that it could be their last chance to make some decent money out of the group. Not that there wasn't friction: the band initially wanted to call the album *"Oklahoma!"* and promotional cassettes were even sent out to the press bearing that title. But, fearing legal action, Capitol insisted on a change, and so the Butthole Surfers went for *Electriclarryland* – a classic rock pun in the style of *Hairway To Steven* that they'd been kicking around for a few years, referencing both Jimi Hendrix's *Electric Ladyland* and the *Larry Sanders Show*, the latest vehicle for comedian Garry Shandling, who had been name-checked on 'Revolution Part Two'.

The album was released In April 1996, and finally gave the band the breakthrough hit they craved: the single 'Pepper', which topped the Billboard Modern Rock charts that summer, as well as reaching number 38 in the mainstream Top 40. The album itself reached number 31 and went gold (shifting over 500,000 units) by August. Its infiltration into the Wal-Mart market was no doubt helped by a "clean" version of the CD that had all profanities removed from the songs and even the band's name censored. Further publicity was gleaned when the band achieved what was surely a longstanding ambition and actually appeared on *The Larry Sanders Show* in January 1997, performing 'Ulcer Breakout'. Tragically, Sanders seemed strangely resistant to the band's entreaties that they hang out together afterwards.

If the success of *Electric Larryland* justified Capitol's faith in the band, then the hits and the way they were achieved also reinforced the scorn of those who shouted sell-out. Indeed, the album itself was a far cry from the Butthole Surfers' sound of yore. *Independent Worm Saloon* may have been expensively produced and relatively straightforward, but it was still a punishing rock record. *Electriclarryland* still had some rockers, but it also contained pop songs, ballads, dance tracks and, in 'Pepper', a hit single that sounded suspiciously like Beck's 1994 breakthrough, 'Loser'. Moreover, none of the songs on *Electriclarryland* had been played live before the album had been released. Every previous Buttholes LP had contained songs that had often been in the band's set for several years before being recorded. Now it seemed like the stockpile of "real" Butthole Surfers songs had been used up. *Electriclarryland* was something new.

But while all of this is true, I'm going to offend the sensibilities of many Butthole Surfers die-hards and suggest that *Electriclarryland* remains a great album – the finest late-period Buttholes' release and their best since *Locust Abortion Technician,* but in a completely different way. In 'Pepper' they shot a genuine Texan psych classic into the Top 40, not only mentioning their home state in the lyrics, but documenting the dark side of the druggy counter-culture in the true 13th Floor Elevators tradition, and providing a suitably disorienting and perception-shifting soundtrack that matched the imagery evoked by the words. *Electriclarryland* may not have been the macho endurance test of the band's earlier albums – you know, "if you can listen to this you're a true freak, man, you're hardcore, this ain't sissy pop music, this twisted noise blast separates the men from the boys." But it performed the classic sleight-of-hand of swaddling extremely dark and difficult songs in accessible melodies and appealing rhythms and, as a result, repaid repeated listens where the true dank depths of the music are revealed.

On the surface, the record is light and catchy, albeit with a distinct air of unease. Dig deeper, though, and the unease grows as the light rapidly dims. For all its dumb humour, its cartoon cover (though check the Elevators-like third eye on the kitsch dog painting on the reverse) and its push for mainstream acceptance, *Electriclarryland* is an album about death, loss of faith, and drugs – specifically, heroin.

"Alright, what are we doing here?" begins 'Birds', a track that seems to be a continuation of *Independent Worm Saloon*, with its dense, industrial rock groove and Gibby's ranting vocal. Its message of cynical apathy and nihilism could easily pass as slacker generation anti-philosophy by numbers, but despite being buried in the mix, the spat-out sentiments of vituperative resignation seem genuine and bitterly heartfelt. The key line, "you always end up wasted," lands heavily with the weight of both its meanings.

The clanging 'Cough Syrup' sounds at first like an inconsequential nursery rhyme with a catchy non-sequitur of a minor key chorus, but as the song progresses, the sinister, desperate undertones gradually become more pronounced. "The summer had been stolen and the bases were all loaded... There was big money on the line... There were no point at all... I can't talk so I guess I got nothing to say... The dogs were gone to feral... His liver had gone hard..." By the time the song moves into its final stretch, with the repeated tag line "I hate cough syrup, don't you?", it's clear that this is a fearsome lament, an agonised howl into the vicious, amoral void of the LA night.

During the early nineties, DXM (Dextromethorphan) became a drug of choice for the grunge generation, and was easily available in the form of over-the-counter cough syrups such as Robitussin Maximum Strength (often shortened to Robo by abusers). A powerful dissociative when taken in large doses, the effects of cough syrup are likened by some to being drunk and stoned at the same time. Others have compared it to ketamine. On the drug advice site EROWID, William E White considers the drug potentially more powerful and dangerous than LSD. On a high dosage he describes possible effects as including "spontaneous memory recall, complex delusions, hallucinations, out-of-body experiences, near-death experiences, and perceived contact with spiritual or even alien entities."

White also writes that "balance and body position sense can be significantly affected, ranging from a mild disturbance (some call it sea legs) to a near-total loss of position and balance sense." This, along with the also-reported side effect of paranoia, perhaps explains the song's chorus ("I can't walk so I guess I'm gonna stay at home / They can have my legs, just leave my mail alone"). On the other hand, Gibby did have his mail opened and scattered on his lawn by an unknown person around this time, and also apparently suffered an illness that caused his leg to swell up so much that it was difficult for him to walk.

Kurt Cobain and Courtney Love were famously both recreational users of cough medicine, although it seems Kurt used a medicine – Hycomine – that didn't contain DXM, but rather a mild opiate that eased his chronic stomach pains. Later, he moved on to heroin for the same analgesic reasons, though for a while this was kept under wraps and his increasing no-shows at scheduled interviews and soundchecks were sometimes put down to his need to secure the right brand of cough syrup. Kurt and Courtney actually met and bonded over their love of cough syrup at a Butthole Surfers show. Many reports on the death of River Phoenix also made a point of stating that cough syrup was one of the substances found in his system on the night that he died, alongside cannabis, Valium, heroin and cocaine. Many tried to suggest that the cough syrup was a major contributory factor to his demise.

The deaths of both Kurt Cobain and River Phoenix must have hit Gibby hard. The former was a younger singer who had been a Butthole Surfers fan, and whose band Nirvana had shared many bills with the Buttholes. Gibby was also one of the last people to see Kurt alive. River too had become a friend of Gibby's, and died outside the Viper Room while Gibby was on stage. These were deaths that profoundly affected a generation, but for Gibby they were also friends who, like him, were struggling with heroin use. They died; Gibby only just survived.

Historically, heroin was first synthesised and patented as a cough medicine, by the international pharmaceutical company Bayer at the end of the nineteenth century. It was sold over the counter till 1914, and finally banned ten years later as the number of addicts grew. This gives us three possibilities as far as the song is concerned. Either Gibby is singing about the use of cough syrup as a recreational drug; he's using "cough syrup" as a code word for heroin; or, more complicatedly, he's commenting ironically on how "cough syrup" becomes a euphemism for other drug problems, and indeed how blaming someone's problems on drugs is a way of avoiding more complex, deeper and troublesome issues: "I hate cough syrup, don't you?"

So when Gibby sings "I heard that your brother was a Viking", he could possibly be referring to Joaquin Phoenix, then known as Leaf, which could easily be misheard as 'Leif' as in Viking explorer Leif Erikson. And "I'd rather be a matchstick than a lighter / I like to see the wood curl up and burn," could conceivably be a riposte to the Neil Young quote in Kurt Cobain's suicide note, "It's better to burn out than fade away." Maybe Gibby would rather slowly frazzle and deteriorate than flare brightly before being suddenly extinguished.

But ultimately this is mere speculation. As the song says, "if you want to know the truth, you've got to dig up Johnny Booth," referring to claims that Abraham Lincoln's assassin, the actor John Wilkes Booth, in fact escaped to Granbury, Texas and lived for many years under an alias, and that the man shot by soldiers outside a burning barn in Virginia was a lookalike. Repeated calls for the body to be exhumed have been rejected; these are mysteries that may never be solved, and one could follow this song deep into the conspiracy theory rabbit hole forever.

Yet despite – or perhaps because of – its ambiguity, 'Cough Syrup' remains a powerful and significant song. Gibby's delivery grows steelier with each line, the edge of bitterness and controlled anger growing. By the time the song fades out into elegiac strings the transition from simple pop song to an elegy for lost souls, and indeed for the soul of America itself, is complete. Or maybe I'm reading far too much into it and it is just about cough syrup, after all. Yeah, I hate that stuff, don't you?

'Pepper' rides in on a classic Buttholes guitar riff, slowed down to half speed for queasy effect, before dropping into a spare, empty hip-hop beat. Gibby's spoken vocals are compressed to sound like he's talking on the phone or the radio, creating an effect of distance and alienation. The misadventures of various teenagers are described in a blank, non-judgemental fashion, merely commenting that "They were all in love with dying / They were doing it in Texas."

Gibby is writing about his generation; specifically, he is writing about his peer group at Lake Highlands High School in Dallas during the early 1970s. "I was also in the class of '76 at Lake Highlands

HS in Dallas, knew Gibby since 5th Grade," wrote one anonymous commentator on the lyrics site Sing365, in a discussion on the meaning of the song. "The first time I heard this song it struck a nerve and I KNEW it was about us."

"I went to high school in Dallas with the lead singer, Gibby Haynes," added another commentator, Bryan. "This song is just a reflection of the people in our high school. Pretty messed up class, I have to say."

The song is straight reportage; the names are not changed, the people are real. Tommy did play piano wonderfully, and lost a leg from an accident on a railroad track. Paulie got shot. Others died from heroin overdoses, or AIDS. But the descriptions of reckless, nihilistic behaviour and near-suicidal risk-taking struck a chord with a wider body of listeners than the original circle described; many who were not yet born when the class of '76 graduated recognised themselves and their friends in the song's lyrics. They, too, were drinking up experience like water from a fountain, till eventually it became an avalanche, crashing down to bury them.

"Everybody has their wild-ass situation where there's a car wreck and a house on fire, and a rape and the strange teacher, and the paedophilia with the wrestling coach," Gibby said. "Everybody's had that shit go down. I think it's pretty cold and clumsy. I wish we'd had more time to work with it."

Only on the chorus does Gibby really allow poetic license to take over. "I don't mind the sun sometimes, the images it shows / I can taste you on my lips and smell you on my clothes / Cinnamon and sugary and softly spoken lies / We never know just how we look through other peoples' eyes." It's been suggested that these lines are about heroin, with its sickly-sweet smell; they could equally be just about memory, the bittersweet emotions it carries and the tricks it plays. Gibby's nasal, finger-in-the-ear delivery is neo-Appalachian, a throwback to Texan bluegrass ballads sung round the hearth or campfire, but underpinned here by psychedelic, reversed guitars. The disorienting effects provide a dream-like contrast to the harsh realism of the lyrics, and a languid fuzz- and wah-drenched solo from Paul winds through chiming, bell-like synthesiser chords as the song fades back into the void from which it's reporting.

The crunching 'Thermador' revolves around a neat, grungy chorus that is both succinct and bleakly existential. "Everybody knows freedom / you find it inside your head," Gibby sings. "Everybody knows Jesus / you meet him when you are dead." The song also quotes Buffalo Springfield's 1966 Sunset Strip protest anthem 'For What It's Worth', applying it to a tougher, nastier era.

'Ulcer Breakout' kicks in with a gloriously greasy fuzz-bass riff before exploding into a gonzo-punk testimonial to the joys of living dangerously, particularly driving stupidly fast, possibly while on drugs. Wonderfully dumb, it's Hunter S Thompson's *Fear And Loathing In Las Vegas* compressed into a two and a half minute song, complete with a speed freak's attention to detail: "Got to be at least 500 inches."

Riding a bass-and-drums groove not dissimilar to Nirvana's 'Come As You Are' but taken up a key, the jangly 'Jingle Of A Dog's Collar' is insidiously catchy, but also oddly unsettling. A funk guitar coda may put the acid-punk crowd's noses out of joint, but actually the structure is not that different to early Buttholes folk-rockers like 'Hey'. Essentially, this is a semi-ironic, self-pitying smack song about how Gibby would pass out on heroin and be woken up by his dog, Mr Cigar, licking his face. Hence, "What do they know about love?" A junkie and his dog, that's true love.

"What it's really about is, waking up on the floor with a dog licking your face, in the bathroom with blood on the ceiling and walls," Gibby told *Rolling Stone*. "Bathtub as a toilet. Fifty gnarly rigs lying everywhere. Dirty dope spoons taped to the wall, made into art pieces. I thought it was a joke."

But 'Jingle Of A Dog's Collar' also functions as a sugary pop song that comments on itself; the lyrics that mouth empty platitudes about love without any meaning or insight, the chorus a predictable hook that excites a Pavlovian response in the listener: "The jingle of a dog's collar would be good right now." Even the sound of the panting hound at the end could just be the audience getting what it wants; a pop song no more significant than a scratch behind the ears.

The country ballad 'TV Star' is played completely straight, despite the blandness of its subject matter screaming "piss-take". Only the uncomfortable pause after Gibby admits "I did something weird" breaks from the soporific formula of plangent slide guitar, busking acoustic, brushed drums and lazy "la la la" chorus. Written about Christina Applegate – still best known as Kelly, the daughter from cynical US sitcom *Married With Children* (1987-1997) – the song also reflects on the vacuity of the celebrity lifestyle, and the weirdness of suddenly hanging out with people you know from TV. Christina Applegate was also famously a witness to River Phoenix's death outside the Viper Room.

The creepy, funny, unsettling 'My Brother's Wife' thankfully snaps us right back into weird Butthole Surfers territory. Conjuring forbidden lust and guilt of Biblical proportions, this Lynchian vignette of suburban dystopia is wreathed in sound effects and echo, layered, trippy and dream-like. Over chattering voices, a synthesised choir of angels and King's insistent drumming – like an anxious, tell-tale heartbeat – Gibby agonises in a mock upper-class English accent that accurately conveys repression and quiet torment: "Sadly I turned to the left, and I see / My brother's wife's breasts / I really must be off / Oh god…"

From this point, the album gradually winds down. 'Ah Ha' begins with the riff to Eddie Cochran's 'Somethin' Else' (via the Sex Pistols' version), before shifting into yet another effortless rock-pop paean to existential boredom, while 'The Lord Is A Monkey' is another twisted Gibby rap on sex, smack and mutilation, with a screaming wind tunnel for a middle eight. 'Let's Talk About Cars' may be about giving up heroin, or just about dying, as Gibby says his farewells over Paul's expressive, elegiac guitar winding slowly through mid-paced drums and French small talk. 'L.A.' is throwaway nineties punk, and 'Space' the obligatory psych-rock freakout to close.

Electriclarryland may have lost the Butthole Surfers some old fans, but they gained plenty of new ones, thanks mainly to 'Pepper', which stayed on heavy rotation on MTV for seven weeks and was 1996's most-played song on alternative rock radio, after years when the group couldn't get any airplay at all, mostly thanks to their name. But, even now they were officially rock stars, plenty hadn't changed. The band were still losing money on tour, despite their huge fees, because of the amount they spent on lights and props and keeping the show on the road. They still felt like they weren't getting any support from their record company. The press had turned against them. The food was still bad in Europe. Plus, no-one could believe that the band's success was down to their own ability and hard work.

"We finally have a hit record, and everyone in the music business is taking credit for it," Paul griped to *Rolling Stone*. "Hundreds of guys going around saying, if I can make a hit for the Butthole Surfers, I can make a hit for you." The band were most pleased to learn that 'Pepper' was the number one song played in Texan titty bars.

In spring 1996 the Butthole Surfers finally went back on the road, temporarily recruiting second guitarist Kyle Ellison and bassist Owen McMahon (Drain, Cherubs). Despite now being professionally handled, it wasn't the easiest tour: Gibby was still recovering from his heroin addiction as well as a hernia operation, and was suffering from a punctured eardrum that made him even more bad-tempered than usual. Paul, meanwhile, was grieving for the Butthole Surfers' one-time sixth member, his pit bull terrier Mark Farner From Grand Funk Railroad.

"She was my reason to keep going for a long time," said Paul. "All I wanted was to make enough money so I could get her a house and back yard." After years of guarding the Butthole Surfers' van during shows, and being the band's default counsellor and stress relief, Farner finally died peacefully at the beginning of 1996 at a decent old age, in the back yard of the Austin house that she and Paul had shared during the dog's happy retirement.

Then, just before the band were due to set out on their lengthy international tour, Paul's mother went into hospital. He knew she was dying. Following a disastrous opening date at Austin City Music Hall, at which everything that could go wrong did go wrong in front of a hometown crowd and a large number of industry guests, Paul attempted to get out of the tour by breaking his hand, slamming his fist into a bathroom door. He broke some bones alright, but his father, the retired Dean of Business, insisted he do the tour anyway: "This is your fifteen-year investment. You've got to go." So Paul did the tour, zonked on painkillers, flying home to San Antonio to be at the hospital whenever he could.

Just after Paul's mother died, at the end of June, his father came to see the Butthole Surfers live for the first time, when they played San Antonio. "I think my dad became genuinely proud," Paul said, obviously feeling a sense of reconciliation and achievement after the show. "He was always supportive. I feel bad that I was a disappointment for a while, but in the long run, I think I gained some respect because I stuck with it."

11

THE LAST ASTRONAUTS

Unfortunately, following the breakthrough success of *Independent Worm Saloon* and *Electriclarryland*, the Butthole Surfers spent the rest of the 1990s largely embroiled in legal action. If the success and slick, commercial sound of 'Pepper' had confirmed the suspicions of those old fans who thought the band sold out when they signed to Capitol, then the Butthole Surfers' lawsuit against their old label, Touch And Go, saw their indie credibility disappear completely down the pan.

The Surfers never signed a contract with Touch And Go; the label released their albums on a handshake deal, and an oral agreement to split net profits fifty-fifty. This worked out fine for a while, and the Buttholes became by far Touch And Go's biggest band, until they decided that they'd outgrown the label, and signed first to Rough Trade, and then to Capitol.

The split was amicable at first, with Touch And Go retaining the rights to the four albums the band released on the label, which stayed in print and continued to sell well. Touch And Go also acted as distributor for King's Trance Syndicate label. But once they were off the label, the Buttholes started to feel that label owner Corey Rusk wasn't doing enough to promote their back catalogue which, while theoretically still available, often couldn't be found in record stores.

The band's manager, Tom Bunch, claimed that this was a deliberate policy on Rusk's part, and in December 1995 the band insisted that if Rusk wasn't going to do any promotion or work on the band's behalf, then the profit split on the back catalogue should be changed from 50-50 to 80-20. Rusk refused, and claimed that he had the right to distribute the Surfers catalogue "in perpetuity." The band responded by demanding that Rusk stop selling their albums immediately, and that he return the master tapes. Rusk refused to talk to Bunch, on the grounds that his arrangement was with Gibby and the band, and that if they wanted to re-negotiate, they should call him. But in 1996, with no response forthcoming, the Butthole Surfers filed a lawsuit against Touch And Go, and in January 1998 won back their masters and copyrights, as well as one hundred thousand dollars in damages.

The suit was filed in Touch And Go's home state of Illinois, where state law regards an oral contract as being over when either party decides that it wants out. But Corey Rusk appealed, claiming that their agreement was permanent and citing the unclear wording of Section 203 of the 1976 copyright act as stating that the minimum term for a grant of copyright is 35 years. He cited the 1993 case of Rano versus Sipa Press in California as precedent. In this case, federal law had established a minimum of 35 years where a photographer had orally granted copyright on photographs to a third party.

Judge Terence Evans for the US Court of Appeals disagreed, saying that the point of Section 203 was to safeguard authors and artists, and that 35 years was clearly intended as the maximum period allowed, even if the artist had orally granted a longer term. In March 1999 he dismissed Touch And Go's claim as without merit. But the damage to the Butthole Surfers' reputation had been done; they were seen to have crippled a pioneering and well-respected independent label – and to have spat in the face of the punk rock community that had supported them when they were starving artists – all in the name of grubbing for an extra buck.

Touch And Go had made it a point of honour to keep lawyers and managers out of the picture, and to operate on a basis of mutual trust. All of its artists were signed on a handshake deal for the same 50-50 split. "In 18 years I've tried hard to only work with people I could be friends with and who could understand how it is I want to work," Corey Rusk commented. "This is the only time I've ended up in court."

Rusk considered permanent rights to distribute the records released on the label a fair return for the extremely generous 50-50 deal; a far better arrangement than any major label would ever offer, though arguably a major label would have greater resources to market those records, and so would in theory see a greater overall return. He allowed that bands had the right to leave the label whenever they chose, but that the records they'd already made remained with Touch And Go.

Rusk was represented in court by former Big Black guitarist-turned-lawyer Santiago Durango, who claimed that the oral contract wasn't taken seriously by the judges because such deals weren't prevalent in the big business world they were used to dealing with. "But they are prevalent in the music industry," he claimed. "Any label in Chicago should be concerned about this."

Rusk had appealed because he thought he was doing the right thing, and also because the label relied upon back catalogue income to continue operating. The Butthole Surfers responded that their livelihood also depended upon their back catalogue, and that they didn't have other bands' work to fall back on, as the label did. King Coffey claimed the band never talked about how long the contract would last for.

"When the agreement was made, the band said, 'Sure, we'll do some records on Touch And Go.' We never had any conversations that were, 'You, Corey, will put this out forever.' We never would have given away perpetual rights to our music to someone we had just met."

Yet within the indie and punk community, the response of Fugazi's Ian McKaye was typical. "Courts are the domain of lawyers," he said. "If you have an oral contract, lawyers don't get paid. It's kind of perfect that a court would be offended by that. But if one party becomes a fucking jerk, no contract is going to help. The Butthole Surfers wanted more money. They let their greed totally upset the balance of the relationship."

"It tore me up to see my name on a lawsuit against a friend," Coffey responded. "I love Touch And Go; they're one of the best labels in the country. I wish the records could have stayed on Touch And Go and made money for Touch And Go."

Leary was less forgiving. "We won a victory for the little guy, and everyone is siding with Exxon," he said. "Wait till someone owns half your ass in perpetuity. And when it's forever, it's all your ass that they own. If Corey had won, it would have fucked every artist this side of Pluto."

The band re-mastered their back catalogue and re-released the albums on their own Latino Buggerveil label, and in 1998 a new Butthole Surfers album finally appeared – sort of. *After The Astronaut* was sent out to the press and industry insiders as a promotional cassette – but then promptly disappeared from any release schedules.

"To this day I'm still not sure whether it was a decision made by our management at the time or by the label," King Coffey told *Billboard* magazine in 2001, when asked why *After The Astronaut* was pulled. "It's too painful to remember," was all Paul Leary would say when asked about the situation for this book. "We went from being able to do whatever we wanted, to having people lined up around the block to tell us how to do it." Some accounts suggest that Capitol changed their mind about releasing the album after receiving almost unanimous negative feedback to the promos it sent out. Others say the band was incensed at Capitol releasing promo cassettes before the album was properly finished.

Certainly, *After The Astronaut* was very different in sound and tone to what anyone expected from the Butthole Surfers. In contrast to the industrial-tinged hard rock of their last two releases, it was a mostly subdued, largely electronic affair, though very much still with a disturbing, psychedelic edge. The near-title track 'The Last Astronaut' casts Gibby as a spaceman returning to an Earth devastated by some mysterious disaster, his spoken word vocals as he realises the extent of the destruction ("My god – is there anyone left?") made all the more chilling by the effect of a radio communicator cutting in and out. Backed by ominous piano and dragging beats, the track is devoid of the Buttholes' usual goofy humour, and comes across as an eerie mix of Godspeed! You Black Emperor and Laurie Anderson.

Elsewhere, 'Imbuya' had a tense gothic-electronic sound similar to Alien Sex Fiend, with overdriven guitars, skittering beats and murky vocals. 'Junky Jenny In Gaytown' was another found piece of Asian pop, tampered with in the style of 'Kuntz', but subtler. 'I Don't Have A Problem' set suggestive sampled radio dialogue – "These girls, they got knives, man / They got knives and daggers" – over bubbling effects and swelling orchestral loops. And the dirty, distorted rock of 'Turkey And Dressing' dissolved into Native American chanting, possibly in an oblique comment on how Thanksgiving is founded on near-genocide. The album took the Buttholes out of the pop-metal cul-de-sac they'd been heading down and updated their trademark unsettling surrealism for the era of computer-generated pop music. It may not have had the wildness of their earlier records, but it found them growing old gracefully, and against all the odds maturing with some dignity.

Of course this wasn't the way it worked out.

Whatever the real reasons for the album being pulled, the relationship between band and label deteriorated, and soon their manager, Tom Bunch, was trying to extricate them from their contract. The projected artwork for *After The Astronaut* ended up being used on an album for Capitol band Marcy Playground (*Shapeshifter*) and, to further complicate matters, the Buttholes then decided that they wanted to stop working with Bunch, who sued them for unpaid commissions. The band counter-sued for conflict of interest and other charges. The situation left them unable to play or record for two years.

"Our manager at the time had fallen off the wagon and our relationship with Capitol got wrecked," Leary says. "We couldn't release any new material for a very long time. That's what happens on major labels. They can sit on you and do nothing while you suffocate."

Finally released from Capitol in September 1999, the Butthole Surfers signed a joint contract with Surfdog Records and Hollywood Records. Their new manager was Surfdog president Dave Kaplan, while Hollywood was a division of Disney – an unlikely choice for the Surfers, perhaps, but the draw was label head Rob Cavallo, a Grammy-winning producer who personally came out to Austin to hang with the band. "We didn't feel slimed after we met him," Leary said, while Gibby claimed that being able to talk to the A&R man on a technical level would improve communications. "Rob brings all of that studio savvy to the table," he commented. "And, of course, the promise of riches beyond our imagination."

The band took the existing recordings of *After The Astronaut* with them, and used these as the basis of the new album. But 'Imbuya', 'Junky Jenny' 'I Don't Have a Problem' and 'Turkey And Dressing' were dropped, and other tracks were remixed and subjected to additional recording and post-production. Several new songs were also added, and the resulting record – now titled *Weird Revolution* – was released on Surfdog/Hollywood in 2001. It was a dog. "Our last album was a nightmare in the making," Paul Leary says. "I can't even utter its name."

The title track, an *After The Astronaut* holdover, is an intermittently inspired manifesto, declaimed to a hip-hop beat and based on a speech by Malcolm X, but altered into a rousing call to arms for the freak nation. The original version was an actual Malcolm X speech with only key words altered – close enough to require permission from the assassinated civil rights leader's estate, which was denied. "I'm into the revolutionary aspects of being weird," Gibby explained. "Let your freak flag fly, that's the concept."

Unfortunately, the band's freak flag wilted almost immediately. 'Shame Of Life' is shameful indeed, a slick, craven piece of commercial pap, co-written with Kid Rock and like a weak imitation of 'Pepper', without any of that song's deceptive depths. 'Dracula From Houston' is even worse, while 'Shit Like That' just sounds like a clueless, watered-down approximation of the drug-fried madness the Buttholes built their reputation on. In this context, two other *After The Astronaut* tracks, 'Venus' and 'Mexico' are merely forgettable and relatively inoffensive, having been polished and remixed to a vapid sheen.

'Intelligent Guy', completely reworked from its *After The Astronaut* incarnation, could almost be forgiven if it was deliberately meant to be so awful, tapping into the turn-of-the-century nu-metal / hip-hop crossover while at the same time being blanker and nerdier than the blankest and nerdiest contemporary college rock (Eels, Cake). This makes it sound far more interesting than it actually is, though; like 'Get Down', it's just bad, lazy pop music, a Frankenstein's Monster that moves and jerks because the nerves are connected up in approximately the right way, but is still completely dead behind the eyes. If Pro-Tooled commercial rock vehicles driven by burnt-out, drug-damaged psycho-nihilist hacks are your bag, then *Weird Revolution* might be for you. Hell, it might just be the sickest record the Butthole Surfers ever made.

And yet... the ambiguous Iraq War commentary 'Jet Fighter' is almost moving, despite its dumb joke ending, and 'The Last Astronaut', though remixed, is still a powerful and sombre piece of work. 'Yentel' is a trippy, unsettling ambient groove, while 'They Came In' remains a solid slab of 'Kashmir'-like psychedelic rock. Perhaps the most frustrating thing of all about *Weird Revolution* is that there's obviously a good album struggling to get out from underneath it. But that album is *After The Astronaut*, a dead duck from three years earlier. *Weird Revolution*, sadly, is just a bad album for bad times.

It also wasn't the hit that the band and their new record company needed, peaking at #130 on Billboard, while 'The Shame Of Life' reached #24 on the Billboard Modern Rock Tracks chart. With Nathan Calhoun on bass and Josh Klinghoffer on second guitar, the *Weird Revolution* tour was also a flop, happening as it did in the wake of 9/11. "People weren't in the mood for mayhem and belching explosions, and neither was I," Leary said. "The road just got to be such a grind. I prefer being here in my house with my wife. I have a life here, and I really like working in the studio where I can be in control of everything that goes on."

After a brief summer tour in 2002, with Nathan Calhoun still on bass but Jason Morales on second drum kit replacing the second guitarist, the Butthole Surfers effectively disappeared. That it was all over wasn't immediately apparent; 2002 saw the release of a "new" album of outtakes and old demos, *Humpty Dumpty LSD*, while in 2003 Latino Buggerveil put out the band's first two EPs on one CD. There was no official announcement of a split, but no-one seemed to have any appetite to continue the band either. Gibby, Paul and King were all well into their forties, and all had other projects to occupy them. Paul Leary became an in-demand producer for the likes of the Bad Livers and the Meat Puppets, while Gibby recorded an album with his new band, Gibby Haynes And His Problem, in 2004.

Although the album was sparse on credits, with songs generally just credited to "The Problem," Gibby's new band featured latter-day Butthole Surfers touring musicians Kyle Ellison (guitar) and Nathan Calhoun (bass), plus drummer Shandon Sahm, son of legendary Texan musician Doug Sahm (The Sir Douglas Quintet), and a bandmate of Ellison's from Texan metal band Pariah and the late nineties incarnation of the Meat Puppets. Shandon's brother Shawn would sing on the track 'Letter' which also featured the Sir Douglas Quintet's Augie Meyers on distinctive organ stabs. Otherwise, keys were played by Laura Scarborough, although Paul Leary added keyboards to the track 'Superman' and mixed five of the album's eleven tracks.

This was a line-up with considerable potential, but the problem with The Problem was that all of their songs sounded like fairly aimless jam sessions, with Gibby improvising vocals as he went along. This needn't be a bad thing; it's how the Butthole Surfers always worked, after all. But with The Problem, that essential spark of madness was missing. The band obviously set out to write commercial rock songs, and these were further smoothed out in the studio and again in the mix, leaving them sounding distinctly phoned in.

'Superman', for instance, sounds weirdly melancholy and detached, like Gibby is floating in a pain-free bubble: "Across the ocean at the light of speed, Superman has killer weed… everything is super, man." The album divides between chugging rockers like 'Kaiser', 'Charlie' and '15000', and chiming folk-rock power ballads like 'Woo' and 'Stop Foolin'. Side two is slightly better than side one: 'Letter' has a vaguely Tex-Mex feel, while the minor-chord hard rock of 'Nights' is well-suited to Gibby's nasal, whinnying vocal style. 'I Need Some Help" is a foggy, slow-psych jam that stretches to eight and a half minutes, with Gibby exhibiting some characteristic wordplay: "I heard the sky and saw the sound." The album ends with the enjoyable goth-rock of 'Dream Machine' and the throwaway Ministry pastiche, 'Redneck Sex'. The latter was reworked by Peaches for a 12" single, making it at least a danceable club track. "Stop acting so crazy," Gibby drawls. But the trouble was that he wasn't acting crazy enough.

SCATOLOGICAL ALCHEMY

It should be said that Gibby Haynes And His Problem worked a whole lot better live. Gibby reintroduced the Gibbytronix, and there was enough chaos and dirt to make the songs sound a lot more exciting and unhinged than on what was ultimately an acceptable but fairly sterile album. Extensive touring and festival appearances may have won the band a greater following, but with scant promotion from Surfdog, Gibby's Problem was soon swept under the carpet for good.

12

THE REVENGE OF ANUS PRESLEY

In many respects the Butthole Surfers story would seem to have ended with the painful, messy birth of the new century. Their brand of psychedelic, psychotic art terrorism belonged to an earlier, less corporate era, and the limping finale of the *Weird Revolution* tour seemed to demonstrate how little they belonged in the cold light of post-9/11 America.

And yet, if the early 21st Century would prove anything, it would be that we are not yet ready to let go of our past idols. No rock band is ever gone for good, until all of the original members are dead, and often not even then. So it should come as no real surprise that, six years after that seemingly final tour, the Butthole Surfers should reform with the 'classic' line-up of Gibby, Paul, King, Jeff and Teresa for a US and European tour. Even Kathleen Lynch turned up to dance – fully clothed – for a handful of dates.

This being the Buttholes however, there was a bizarre twist. The tour would be undertaken in tandem with the Paul Green School Of Rock Music. Musician Paul Green had formed the school in his native Philadelphia in 1998, and quickly developed it into a wildly successful after-school program with franchises across America. The School Of

Rock took youngsters of any skill level and taught them how to play the instrument of their choice, forming them into bands with the aim of getting them onstage in concert before a paying audience. The program inspired both the documentary *Rock School* and, allegedly, the hit comedy *School Of Rock* starring Jack Black.

In 2007 Green staged the first School Of Rock Festival in Asbury Park, New Jersey, a two-day event that was headlined by Ween and Bad Brains, alongside sets from the School Of Rock All-Stars – bands featuring top of the class kids from School of Rock programs around the states. It was Ween bassist Dave Dreiwitz who first approached Gibby Haynes about working with the School Of Rock; specifically, he thought it would be an amazing thing for Gibby to do a Butthole Surfers set with a bunch of Green's teenage All-Stars.

The result was a five-date tour of the Eastern United States in February 2008, billed as the Paul Green School Of Rock featuring Gibby Haynes. Backed by a revolving cast of capable All-Stars in their early teens, Gibby performed a career-spanning set of Butthole Surfers songs, and by all accounts appeared to be having more fun than he'd enjoyed in years. Lights, strobes, smoke and projections were employed in an attempt to give the shows an authentic feel, although halfway through Gibby would leave the stage for an interlude in which the School Of Rock All-Stars performed their own material.

Having relearned his own songs from the rock kids during long rehearsals for the short tour, it seems Gibby was keen that this effort not be wasted and pulled the rest of the Butthole Surfers into the fold. King Coffey and Jeff Pinkus quickly agreed, and Teresa re-joined them after playing live for the first time in over a decade that Spring, with King's experimental psychedelic band Rubble. Since undergoing brain surgery in 1993, Teresa had made a slow, difficult recovery, and was still taking anti-epileptic medication while dealing with anxiety issues. Nevertheless, she felt the time was right to resume her double drumming tag team with King.

The final member of the Butthole Surfers to agree to play the shows was Paul Leary. Although he still loved playing music and working in the studio, he was reluctant to play live again. Indeed, his participation in the summer 2008 tour was only confirmed at the last minute, and he claims that he finally consented "in a weak moment". And although the hook-up with the School Of Rock just seemed wrong on many levels for the Butthole Surfers, it may have been the factor that finally swung Leary in favour of accepting. "Everything the Butthole Surfers have ever done has been pretty bizarre," he told the *Austin Chronicle's* Margaret Moser. "From that point of view, this seems to fit right in, and it probably wouldn't have happened any other way."

Maybe the presence of the School Of Rock All-Stars on the tour also helped Gibby and the others avoid the idea that this was a reunion, a word all were decidedly reluctant to countenance. Certainly the rock kids weren't necessary to sell tickets: seeing the classic Buttholes line-up perform live again for the first time since the 1980s would have been a big enough draw in its own right for thousands of fans, both veterans of the post-punk underground and younger fans who grew up hearing legendary tales of abandon and debauchery. As it was, the School Of Rock opened most shows and then a rotating cast of All-Stars backed the Buttholes on stage throughout their set, although apparently their involvement would vary from show to show. The concerts would generally climax with all of the kids joining the Buttholes for a rousing rendition of 'The Shah Sleeps In Lee Harvey's Grave' that was crazy enough to make you suspect that this was how the song should always have been performed.

An exception was the final US date, at New York's Webster Hall on July 29. Here Gibby was escorted offstage towards the end of the band's set by security after getting into an argument with the venue's sound engineer. When the rest of the band followed, the audience started booing and throwing bottles on stage, and scuffles with the allegedly heavy-handed security started to break out. Psychic TV's Genesis P Orridge took to the stage to appeal for calm until he, too, was bundled off by the bouncers. It was at least a small reminder of the chaos and antagonism the Buttholes once routinely inspired.

The European dates also had their share of mayhem, and the Butthole Surfers managed to get banned for life from playing any All Tomorrow's Parties events, albeit briefly. The band (now without the School Of Rock All-Stars) played at the 'Nightmare Before Christmas' edition of the festival curated by the Melvins and Mike Patton, in

December 2008. After Gibby had passed out in the cafeteria he was rudely awakened and asked to leave. All hell inevitably broke loose, resulting in a statement from ATP boss Barry Hogan that the Butthole Surfers would never play the festival again, and that they could "suck my balls". A couple of years later, however, Hogan did try to re-book the Buttholes. Leary enquired if he still required the band to suck his balls, and Hogan apologised.

Minus the All-Stars, the Butthole Surfers played extensively across America, Europe and Canada in 2009. In 2010 they performed *Locust Abortion Technician* in its entirety at the first of two Halloween shows at Austin's Scoot Inn, followed by two New Year's Eve shows in Brooklyn. 2011 saw Gibby, Paul, King and Jeff play a 12-date US tour, winding up in Austin on September 11.

After that, the Butthole Surfers went their separate ways again. Jeff Pinkus remained the most active. He had formed Honky in the late nineties, following the split of his previous post-Buttholes band, Daddy Longhead, and immediately resumed working with the uncomplicated hard boogie trio. In 2016 they released their fifth album, *Corduroy,* and promoted it with a US and European tour. While continuing to lead Honky's southern rock boogie assault on his distinctive Flying V bass, in 2013 Pinkus also joined the Melvins as one of their regular rotating bass players. The Melvins' 2014 album *Hold It In* also featured Paul Leary, who played guitar and co-wrote three songs on the album, leading many to describe the temporary line-up as a Melvins/Butthole Surfers supergroup.

Leary formed the "psychedelic blues" band Carny in 2003, with Sam McCandless and Formica. The trio played live intermittently and reportedly recorded an album, but at the time of writing it has yet to see the light of day. In 2015 they changed their name to the Cocky Bitches, and Leary remains easily distracted by TV sports, *Judge Judy* and production work for California punk band Sublime With Rome, among others.

Rubble, featuring King Coffey on drums alongside singer-bassist Matt Turner and guitarists Bobby Baker and Shawn McMillen, released their album *The Farewell Drugs* on Latino Buggerveil in 2011. Finally, Gibby contributed backing vocals to a couple of Psychic

TV albums in the late noughties and produced the Lemonheads' covers album *Varshons* in 2009. In 2013 he released a single on Jack White's Third Man label, a cover of 'Paul's Not Home' by Adrenalin O.D., and in 2015 he joined heavy rock band Mastodon on their single 'Atlanta'.

On December 18th 2016, the Butthole Surfers played their first show for over five years at Houston's Day For Night festival. Slick, arty, expensive, strictly policed and hipster-friendly, this was very much a 21st century music fest, combining a self-consciously eclectic music program with immersive art installations and a strong emphasis on cutting edge digital technology, all set in a vast abandoned post office/brutalist warehouse space. Besides the Buttholes, the three-day event also featured Aphex Twin, Squarepusher, Bjork, the Jesus & Mary Chain, Run The Jewels, Ariel Pink, film director and composer John Carpenter and many other artists and performers. The Butthole Surfers were the penultimate act on the second stage on the final day, sandwiched between Unknown Mortal Orchestra and acclaimed Houston hip-hop artist Travis Scott.

Greying, bespectacled and wrapped in thick hoodies against the December cold, the four-piece line-up of Gibby, Paul, Jeff and King were joined for 'The Shah Sleeps In Lee Harvey's Grave' by Gibby's young son Satchel, playing stand-up snare and cymbal in a padded yellow anorak and ear protectors at the front of the stage, while King hammered a full kit behind. Gibby broke off from manipulating his Gibbytronix halfway through to hug his boy, who shrugged off the fatherly embrace to resume drumming in perfect time. The band played a well-received forty-minute set, including respectable versions of most of their key songs, from 'Lady Sniff' to 'Pepper'. But the spirit of Anus Presley that originally animated this most monstrous and perverse of bands appeared to be long absent. It would be completely understandable if the Butthole Surfers of 2016 had no desire to reanimate it.

The rock'n'roll demon that Gibby Haynes and Paul Leary summoned up in San Antonio in 1981 possessed them, and the other players that joined the Butthole Surfers along the way, for roughly a decade. The majority of those ten years were spent in conditions of poverty and degradation, of self-inflicted mental and physical torture, oscillating between psychic extremes, while being constantly punished by hunger, brutality and exhaustion. But out of this suffering came some of the greatest and most crazed live performances ever seen in the rock music era.

Both practical magic and great rock'n'roll are powered by extreme emotional states. Sex and drugs are powerful shortcuts, but anger, fear, pain and ecstatic excitement can also drive the engine. Great magicians, like Aleister Crowley, often end their days in poverty and disgrace, much to the bemusement of observers, who may reasonably ask, If you're such a great wizard, how come you've so comprehensively failed at life?

Great rock'n'rollers often enjoy more substantial material rewards, though a stable family life and comfortable longevity can similarly elude them. It also seems to be the case that once they have 'made it' and seen the rewards of their labours, the quality of their art takes a notable downturn. Even those artists who never enjoy major success find it hard to sustain their chaotic, demanding muse into middle age. This is not so often the case with musicians and composers in other fields, or for authors, playwrights, film directors, painters, sculptors or actors. Most artists in most fields improve and deepen in their work as they grow older and more experienced. Magicians and rock'n'rollers seem to be the exception.

The Butthole Surfers became notorious for a lifestyle that only young men and women could endure, and created great art that was inextricably bound up with that lifestyle. Indeed, the songs and the records almost seemed like accidental by-products of the band's chaotic touring lifestyle, fully formed moments of unintentionally revealing genius that the band dismissed as crap because they occurred almost without their agency. They focussed instead on the performance, and somehow not only got out alive but achieved a considerable measure of fame and financial reward as a result. At which point their destructive, amoral, chaotic demon-muse deserted them, and one suspects they were not all that disappointed to see it go.

As Paul and Gibby drift into their sixties, they don't need to suffer for their art anymore. They don't want to set themselves on fire, or go for a week without food or sleep, or snort up a lethal combination of drugs just in order to put on the shows and come up with the songs that made their name. The Butthole Surfers have done their time in hell, and are entitled to their victory laps, their quiet family lives, their afternoon soaps and home studio hobby bands.

The spirit of Anus Presley is elsewhere. Rock'n'roll itself may be a rapidly discredited twentieth century art form and ideology, but somewhere in the underground it is still alive. For every fifth generation punk or noise band, every dysfunctional abuser of electronic instrumentation, every rapper or poet allowing themselves uncensored access to their darkest and most taboo thoughts and desires, the spirit of Anus Presley is waiting; waiting to serve you; waiting to take possession; waiting to take revenge.

Original Butthole Surfers founder member Scott Mathews sadly died in 2010. To the best of my knowledge, at the time of writing, all the other Butthole Surfers are all still alive.

BUTTHOLE SURFERS DISCOGRAPHY

Untitled EP, AKA *Brown Reasons To Live*, AKA *Pee-Pee The Sailor* (Alternative Tentacles, 1983)
The Shah Sleeps In Lee Harvey's Grave / Hey / Something / Bar-B-Q Pope / Wichita Cathedral / Suicide / The Revenge Of Anus Presley

Live PCPPEP (Alternative Tentacles, 1984)
Cowboy Bob / Bar-B-Q Pope / Dance Of The Cobras / The Shah Sleeps In Lee Harvey's Grave / Wichita Cathedral / Hey / Something

Psychic... Powerless... Another Man's Sac (Touch And Go, 1984)
Concubine / Eye Of The Chicken / Dum Dum / Woly Boly / Negro Observer / Butthole Surfer / Lady Sniff / Cherub / Mexican Caravan / Cowboy Bob / Gary Floyd

Cream Corn From The Socket Of Davis (Touch And Go, 1985)
Moving To Florida / Comb / To Parter / Tornadoes

Rembrandt Pussyhorse (Touch And Go, 1986)
Creep In The Cellar / Sea Ferring / American Woman / Waiting For Jimmy To Kick / Strangers Die Every Day / Perry / Whirling Hall Of Knives / Mark Says Alright / In The Cellar

BUTTHOLE SURFERS DISCOGRAPHY

Locust Abortion Technician (Touch And Go, 1987)
Sweat Loaf / Graveyard / Pittsburgh To Lebanon / Weber / Hey / Human Cannonball / USSA / The O-Men / Kuntz / Graveyard / 22 Going On 23

Hairway To Steven (Touch And Go, 1988)
Jimi / Ricky / I Saw An X-Ray Of A Girl Passing Gas / John E Smoke / Roky / Julio Iglesias / Backass / Fart Song

Widowmaker (Touch And Go, 1989)
Helicopter / Bong Song / The Coloured FBI Guy / Booze Tobacco Dope Pussy Cars

Double Live (Latino Buggerveil, 1989)
To Parter / Psychedelic Jam / Ricky / Roky / Gary Floyd / Florida / John E Smoke / Tornadoes / Pittsburgh To Lebanon / The One I Love / Graveyard / Sweat Loaf / Backass / Paranoid / Fast / I Saw An X-Ray Of A Girl Passing Gas / Strawberry / Jimi / Lou Reed

'The Hurdy Gurdy Man' / 'Barking Dogs' (Rough Trade single, 1990)

Piouhgd (Rough Trade, 1991)
Revolution Part 1 / Revolution Part 2 / Lonesome Bulldog / Lonesome Bulldog II / The Hurdy Gurdy Man / Golden Showers / Lonesome Bulldog III / Blindman / No, I'm Iron Man / Something / P.S.Y. / Lonesome Bulldog IV

Independent Worm Saloon (Capitol, 1993)
Who Was In My Room Last Night? / The Wooden Song / Tongue / Chewin' George Lucas' Chocolate / Goofy's Concern / Alcohol / Dog Inside Your Body / Strawberry / Some Dispute Over T-Shirt Sales / Dancing Fool / You Don't Know Me / The Annoying Song / Dust Devil / Leave Me Alone / Edgar / The Ballad of Naked Man / Clean it Up

'Good King Wencenslaus' / 'The Lord Is A Monkey' (Trance Syndicate single, 1994)

The Whole Truth... And Nothing Butt (Trance Syndicate, 1995)
Butthole Surfer / Something / Moving To Florida / Hurdy Gurdy Man / Come Together / Cherub / Graveyard / USSA / Lady Sniff / John E Smoke / 1401 / Psychedelic Jam / Bong Song / Pittsburgh To Lebanon / The Shah Sleeps In Lee Harvey's Grave / WNYU Interview

Electriclarryland (Capitol, 1996)
Birds / Cough Syrup / Pepper / Thermador / Ulcer Breakout / Jingle Of A Dog's Collar / My Brother's Wife / Ah Ha / The Lord Is A Monkey / Let's Talk About Cars / L.A. / Space

'Pepper (single edit)' / 'Pepper (Butcher Bros remix)' (Capitol single, 1996)

The Last Astronaut (Capitol, 1998; unreleased)
The Weird Revolution / Intelligent Guy / Jet Fighter / Imbuya / Mexico / Venus / The Last Astronaut / Yentel / Junkie Jenny From Gaytown / They Came In / I Don't Have A Problem / Turkey & Dressing

Weird Revolution (Hollywood Records, 2001)
The Weird Revolution / The Shame Of Life / Dracula From Houston / Venus / Shit Like That / Mexico / Intelligent Guy / Get Down / Jet Fighter / The Last Astronaut / Yentel / They Came In

Humpty Dumpty LSD (Latino Buggerveil, 2002)
Night Of The Day / 100 Million People Dead / I Love You Peggy / Space 1 / Perry Intro / Day Of The Dying Alive / Chicken Eindhoven Masque / Just A Boy / Sinister Crayon / Hetero Skeleton / Earthquake / Ghandi / I Hate My Job / Space 2 / Concubine Solo / All Day / Sherman / DADGAD

Live At The Forum London (Live Here Now, 2008)
22 Going On 23 / Fast Song / Suicide / Moving To Florida-100 Million People Dead / Some Dispute Over T-Shirt Sales / Goofy's Concern / To Parter-Tornadoes / 1401 / Graveyard / Dust Devil / Ulcer Breakout / Roky / Cowboy Bob / Cherub / Sweat Loaf / I Saw An X-Ray Of

BUTTHOLE SURFERS DISCOGRAPHY

A Girl Passing Gas / Gary Floyd-Jimi Part 1 / Jimi Part 2-Cartoon / Happy Birthday (Mariella and Gianni) / The Shah Sleeps In Lee Harvey's Grave

BIBLIOGRAPHY / NOTES

Chapter 2 – The Peppermint Punk

The quotes from Scott Mathews are taken from a 2001 interview by Chris Smart, archived on the 'Anal Obsession' Butthole Surfers fan site (http://buttholesurfersao.blogspot.co.uk/2010/03/rip-scott-mathews.html). This site has been an invaluable aide, and throughout this book I've relied extensively on their gigography (www.buttholesurfersanalobsession.com) and two articles detailing the different line-ups of the band (http://buttholesurfersao.blogspot.co.uk/2009/06/line-up.html and http://buttholesurfersao.blogspot.co.uk/2009/06/line-up-part-2-electric-boogerloo.html).

Gibby Haynes: "It was badass...", Jello Biafra: "The weirdest homemade zine", Paul Leary: "We'd start practicing..." and "It was more of a performance piece..." from 'Feeding The Fish: An Oral History of the Butthole Surfers', by Joe Nick Patowski and John Morthland, *Spin* magazine November 1996.

Paul Leary: "He had a nice stereo...", "I was free to pursue..." and "Gibby had to really beg me..." from an email interview conducted by the author.

Gibby Haynes: "One of the main themes was how horrible music was back then...", *Caught In The Crossfire* interview, September 2004. http://www.caughtinthecrossfire.com/music/gibby-haynes-butthole-surfers-interview/

Margaret Moser: "The Sex Pistols left no unfinished business..." from 'Holiday In San Antonio' by Margaret Moser, *The Austin Chronicle*, January 10, 2003.

Chapter 3 – Weird Shit

Paul Leary: "We started out as the Dick Clark Five...", Quinn Matthews: "They were doing a lot of TV songs..." and King Coffey: "We went down to Austin..." from 'Feeding The Fish' as above.

Scott Mathews quotes from Anal Obsession interview as above.

Gibby Haynes: "They hated us there...", "Everybody hated us..." and Paul Leary: "Then we realised we couldn't get jobs..." from an interview in *Forced Exposure* #11, winter 1987 by Jimmy Johnson and Byron Coley.

King Coffey: "Trying to be the most psychedelic band..." and "The worst bathroom crank ever..." from a 2006 interview by Max Dropout chronicling the history of the Hugh Beaumont Experience.

Paul Leary: "It was a demo kind of studio..." from author's own interview.

Chapter 4 – Freak Party

Paul Leary: "I remember calling alternative tentacles..." and "Bob O'Neill started engineering..." from author's own interview

Teresa Taylor: "I was 22 years old..." from 'Feeding The Fish'.

Terence Smart: "I guess I'd had enough by then..." from a 2001 interview with his brother Chris for Anal Obsession (http://www.buttholesurfersanalobsession.com/show. php?era=80&year=1985&id=131)

Chapter 5 – Electric Poison

Gibby Haynes: "Ten minutes into the show..." from 'Gibby Haynes: Don't Try This At Home', interview by Mark Kemp, *Options* magazine #52, Sept/Oct 1993

Paul Leary: "It's really fuckin' hideous" from *Our Band Could Be Your Life* by Michael Azarrad, Back Bay Books, 2001.

Chapter 6 – Satan! Satan! Satan!

Jeff Pinkus: "I lived in the master bedroom closet..." and "We had a Sony Betamax..." from 'Feeding The Fish'.

Jeff Pinkus: "Sandra had a crush on Teresa..." from the 2001 Chris Smart interviews on Anal Obsession (http://www.buttholesurfersanalobsession.com/show. php?era=80&year=1986&id=164)

Chapter 7 – Crazy Goddamn World

Jennie Howell: "A compelling..." author's own interview.

Jim Fedrick: "I'd been to Big Black..." author's own interview.

Chapter 8 – Weed For Weasels

Teresa Taylor: "I'd developed a really big fear of flying..." from 'Out of the Mouths of Children: The Improbable Return of the Butthole Surfers' by Austin Powell, *The Austin Chronicle*, September 26 2008.

Paul Leary: "We had to claw and fight for everything…" from 'Touch And Go v The Buttholes' by Josh Goldfein, *The Chicago Reader*, April 15 1999.

Gibby Haynes: "We're going to go out and get fucked" from *How Soon Is Now? The Madmen And Mavericks Who Made Independent Music 1975-2005* by Richard King, Faber and Faber, 2012.

Gibby Haynes: "But we fucked it up totally…" from 'Journey To The Sphincter Of Your Mind Or… Cowabunghole!' by Peter Orr, *Reflex* magazine, September/October 1991

Brent Grulke: "Blood's spewing everywhere…" from 'Feeding The Fish'.

Gibby Haynes: "It was a joke on Rough Trade…" from 'The Hole Truth and Nothing Butt' by Carlos Nunez, *Fiz* magazine, 1993.

Chapter 9 – Clean It Up

Gibby Haynes: "He's just one of those people who haunt me" and "Cops think like Willie Nelson's on the bus…" from 'Journey To The Sphincter Of Your Mind'

Paul Leary: "Lollapalooza was the first time…", "We made a bunch of money…" and "It was life threatening…", King Coffey: "It was my New Year's resolution…", Margaret Moser: "This was when Ministry was thinking…" and "He'd walk into the Black Cat…", Hale Milgrim: "I knew that we would have some problems…", Jerry Haynes: "I called the station…", Tim Devine: "It was just a matter of making…" and Gibby Haynes: "We were playing a song…" from 'Feeding The Fish'.

Gibby Haynes: "Jesus Built My Hotrod…" from an interview by Mark Rowland on *Penny Black Music*, August 18 2004 (http://www.pennyblackmusic.co.uk/MagSitePages/Article/3419/Gibby-Haynes).

Al Jourgensen: "Gibby came down completely drunk..." from an interview by Dan Macintosh, February 18 2012, archived at http://www.songfacts.com/blog/interviews/al_jourgensen_of_ministry/

Gibby Haynes: "I was too fucked up..." from 'Out Of The Mouths Of Children'.

Robin Hurley: "I would pick up the phone..." from *How Soon Is Now?*

Paul Leary: "A cool dude..." from author's own interview.

Paul Leary: "John Motherfucking Jones" from 'The Hole Truth And Nothing Butt'.

Gibby Haynes: "He was like a horrible drunk..." from *Caught In The Crossfire*.

Chapter 10 – You Always End Up Wasted

Paul Leary: "He came into the studio..." and "Gary kind of freaked me out..." from author's own interview.

William E White: "Spontaneous memory recall..." from the Erowid psychoactive substances information website, https://www.erowid.org/chemicals/dxm/faq/dxm_experience.shtml#toc.5.

"I was also in the class of '76..." and "I went to high school in Dallas..." from comments on lyric site Sing365, http://www.sing365.com/music/lyric.nsf/Pepper-lyrics-Butthole-Surfers/1B93E4B36CC553B348256D0A00310B24

Gibby Haynes: "Everybody has their wild-ass situation..." and "What it's really about...", Paul Leary: "We finally had a hit record...", "She was my reason to keep going...", "This is your fifteen year investment" and "I think my dad became genuinely proud..." from 'Where Would

The Beatles Be Today If They Called Themselves The Butthole Surfers?' by Charles M Young, *Rolling Stone,* January 1996.

Chapter 11 – The Last Astronauts

Corey Rusk: "In 18 years…", Santiago Durango: "But they are prevalent…", King Coffey: "When the agreement was made…", "It tore me up…" and "To this day…", Ian MacKaye: "Courts are the domain of lawyers…" and Paul Leary: "We won a victory…" from 'Touch And Go v The Buttholes'.

Paul Leary: "It's too painful…", "Our manager at the time…" and "Our last album was a nightmare…" from author's own interview.

Paul Leary: "We didn't feel slimed…" and Gibby Haynes: "Rob brings all of that studio savvy…" from 'Butthole Surfers Resurface' by Charles M Young, *Billboard* magazine, September 11 1999.

Gibby Haynes: "I'm into the revolutionary aspects of being weird" from the Hollywood Records press release for *Weird Revolution.*

Paul Leary: "People weren't in the mood…" from 'Out Of The Mouths Of Children'.

Chapter 12 – The Revenge of Anus Presley

Paul Leary: "Everything the Butthole Surfers have ever done…" from 'Out Of The Mouths Of Children'.

www.eleusinianpress.co.uk

#0004 - 090818 - C0 - 229/152/7 - PB - 9781909494169